Money Box

Money Box

✓ *Balancing your budget*

✓ *Growing your bank balance*

✓ *Living a better financial life*

PAUL LEWIS

1

BBC Books, an imprint of Ebury Publishing
20 Vauxhall Bridge Road,
London SW1V 2SA

BBC Books is part of the Penguin Random House group of companies whose addresses can be found at global.penguinrandomhouse.com

This book is published to accompany the radio series entitled *Money Box*, broadcast on BBC Radio 4.

First published by BBC Books in 2023

www.penguin.co.uk

A CIP catalogue record for this book is available from the British Library

ISBN 9781785947070

Printed and bound in Great Britain by Clays Ltd, Elcograf S.p.A.

Penguin Random House is committed to a sustainable future for our business, our readers and our planet. This book is made from Forest Stewardship Council® certified paper.

CONTENTS

INTRODUCTION

This book is about how to get more money, how to stop wasting money, and how to use the money you have better. It covers help from the government or local council. Emergency help from charities or others. Using your skills to make money for yourself. Stopping paying for daft things. And making the money you have work for you not someone else. Pay less tax to the state, beat the banks at their own game, and treat the finance industry not like a friend but more like a vague acquaintance you don't really trust but have to see from time to time and who always makes you pay for the drinks.

It will arm you with the knowledge you need. And warn you about things that can leap up and bite you as well, of course, as those that stealthily drain your money away.

How to use this book

The book is arranged in a new way – like your life. It begins when you are born and ends when, well, you know when. Of course, some things like fraud, investing and falling in love can happen at any age, so they get their own special interludes. Early chapters about finance for babies and children are aimed at their parents – sorry little ones, but you are allowed to read them too, so you know what they are planning for you! And occasionally topics spill over from one age to the other each with its own spin. There will be some duplication because some things are so important they need saying twice, at least. But broadly the chapters follow you through life and explain what you need to know or do in the seven ages of people. And at the end – of the book! – there is a quick reminder about the things you should have done earlier and a handy wormhole to crawl back in time to do them before it's too late!

Handy references to further help, organisations, maybe even the odd book are scattered through the text but are brought together in one place at the back – and to keep you completely up to date I am on Twitter @paullewismoney with my daily news about finance and other things.

A quick word about places

The UK is England, Scotland, Wales and Northern Ireland – I always put them in order of population size. Great Britain is England, Scotland and Wales. Generally, laws and legal procedures are the same in England and Wales though in some matters – the health service, local government and now a few benefits issues – Wales is growing apart thanks to devolution. Money matters are slightly different in Northern Ireland, which is of course not a country – my Northern Irish colleagues tell me – more a province. And several key money facts, including tax and benefits, are often very different in Scotland as the Scottish government flexes its devolution muscles. Long before that, when the English and Scottish governments merged in 1707, Scotland sensibly kept its own education and legal systems, which accounts for some of the differences in student finance and things like wills and divorce law. If I do not mention differences, I am referring to the whole of the UK. But do not confuse that with the British Isles, which includes the Isle of Man and the Channel Islands (principally Jersey and Guernsey), which all have separate governments with their own parliaments. These make their own laws and have their own taxes, benefits, and financial regulators. They are not covered in this book. But the Isle of Wight and the Scilly Isles are part of the UK, as are Shetland and Orkney – and the Isle of Lewis where, before you ask, I do not come from.

Disclaimer

Everything in this book I believed to be correct when I wrote it. Then I checked and made any necessary changes. The great people at Penguin Random House have been all over it too and found other points to correct or clarify – or delete. But there may be things we all missed, or which have changed in ways we didn't expect. Or I may have just expressed something so badly that you misunderstood it. For all of that, I apologise and take full responsibility. Be aware that benefits normally increase each April – this book uses the rates for 2022/23. They should be higher in 2023/24, but may not rise fully with inflation. Tax allowances normally also change then. As I write the final draft of this book there is a freeze on most tax allowances, with no changes due until April 2026. But that is a political decision and as this book was being finalised the UK was plunged into a period of political and economic turmoil. The country had three Prime Ministers and four Chancellors in as many months. Plans for taxes, benefits, and other policies changed, changed back, and changed again. As a result of this chaos, the interest rates paid on savings accounts and charged on mortgages shot up to their highest levels for fifteen years. To keep up with those unprecedented times numerous amendments to the book were made right up to the day of printing at the end of October. So if the details of tax and benefits are different from April 2023 to what was expected or the rates I have quoted on savings or mortgages look silly, forgive me. They were correct at the end of October 2022 just as the new Prime Minister Rishi Sunak was appointed. All the rest of the book remains as true as ever.

Oh, and although I do give advice, quite a lot of it, it is not regulated advice and you should always check it before doing anything that could cost you money. I cannot take any responsibility for money you lose as a result of doing what I suggest. But I will take great joy in money you save or make by living your life in the way I set out – from 0 to 99 and beyond.

CHAPTER 1

BIRTH AND BEFORE

If you sat down and worked out the cost of a baby before you got pregnant, well, you'd probably choose to remain childless. Child Poverty Action Group reckoned in 2021 that it would cost a couple £161,000 to raise their firstborn to adulthood. It would cost a lone parent £194,000. Happily, the financial toll is rarely at the forefront of your mind when you make a baby, which is probably just as well! But as you start bringing them up, you soon realise the cost.

BUDGETING FOR A BABY

There are things you can do to reduce the outlay:

Choose second-hand (not babies, equipment!) where you can, given that babies use highly specialised bits of kit for just a few months before graduating to the next expensive step of development.

Purchasing baby bundles – a collection of second-hand clothes – is another way to reduce costs. And if you do buy new, then sell stuff on when it is past its use-by size.

As with most things financial, I suggest setting up a spreadsheet – I really don't believe you can understand things you can't measure or count – and enter all those essentials so you know what costs to expect at the end of pregnancy, without the frills. And a spreadsheet is just a good way to make lists and organise them, even if you don't use its ability to do sums.

All this big spending on the smallest person in the house comes just at the time when earnings might well be sacrificed to give you bonding time – or just enough sleep. You need to make sure you get as much money as you are entitled to receive.

PREGNANCY SUPPORT

This century, much of the government support for pregnant women has been cut or ended. But here's a quick guide to the remnants. If you are claiming universal credit (see page 102 for more on universal credit) or other means-tested benefits, then you may be able to get a Healthy Start card, which you can use to buy things like milk, fruit, vegetables or beans and you can also get free vitamins – great news because those cost a lot of money and they are good for pregnant women and their babies – see **healthystart.nhs.uk**.

England, Wales and Northern Ireland

A helpful £500 can be had from the Sure Start maternity grant. There are two conditions:

- You only get it for your first child. If you already have children under 16, forget it. But there are exceptions, for example, if second time around you find yourself expecting twins.

AND

- You – or your partner if you have one – must get a means-tested benefit such as universal credit (see box below for a list).

turn2us.org.uk has a great guide to what you can get. Search 'Sure Start grant'.

Scotland

Things are better in Scotland. (I'm tempted to abbreviate that sentence in future to TABIS because they usually are.) There you get a Best Start grant of £642.35 for your first child (twins get one each) and £321.20 for others. Apply from 24 weeks pregnant to when the babe is six months old. There are further payments at two and school age. More on those later – patience, we're before birth here.

Means-tested benefits – these benefits are related to your income and circumstances

- universal credit
- income-based jobseeker's allowance
- income-related employment and support allowance
- income support
- housing benefit
- child tax credit
- working tax credit
- pension credit

They often act as a gateway to other benefits.

Like the rest of the UK, the Best Start grants are only paid to parents who get a means-tested benefit.

If you get a Best Start grant, then you can also get Best Start foods payments. They are £18 a week (paid with a card that operates either contactless or with chip and pin) from pregnancy until your child is three and double that in the child's first year. It's a useful amount of money but comes with strings. And not cheese strings because you can only use the card to buy what the Scottish Government says are 'healthy' foods for you or your baby. These include fresh milk, formula, fresh fruit and eggs.

Further information

A national charity called Working Families has a really useful maternity calendar setting out your rights to help and money week by week. On the back is a new baby calendar.

workingfamilies.org.uk search 'maternity calendar'. It is definitely 'print off and stick it on the wall' stuff.

Disclaimer

The rules about state benefits are very complex and this book doesn't cover every detail (the book that does is nearly 2000 pages long in very small type). So, check the detailed rules at **gov.uk** and then search, for example, 'Sure Start grant'. In Scotland, go to **mygov.scot** and search. In Northern Ireland, it's **nidirect.gov.uk**. Assume that Wales is the same as England. Unless of course, I say it is not. Which it sometimes isn't. It's at **gov.wales**. I will also give other links to further information as we go along.

MATERNITY LEAVE

Most women work during pregnancy until about a month before the baby is due. You can take up to a year off work if you can afford it, but you are only paid for the first nine months (39 weeks). You get 90 per cent of your pay for six weeks and for the rest you get statutory maternity pay – it increases each year but is equivalent to around 16½ hours on the National Living Wage, which is the official minimum wage paid to people aged 23 or more. As I write in 2022, it is £156.66 a week. Your employer pays it. Of course, if your weekly pay is less than that then you only get your weekly pay!

Some employers may pay more than this – full pay for six months, for example. That will be in your employment contract. If it is not, then you will get the standard amounts.

If your employer doesn't pay maternity pay – they've gone bust, for example – or you're self-employed, you get a maternity allowance from the state, paid fortnightly or four-weekly, which is also normally £156.66 a week. But even this is hedged round with all sorts of rules about National Insurance contributions you have paid, so you may not get even that. Again, go to **gov.uk** and search 'maternity allowance'. It is the same throughout the UK. Paternity pay for fathers or same sex partners ditto.

No matter how much you are feeling like it, you can't start your pregnancy leave until 11 weeks before your due date. However, if the baby is born early or you are affected by an illness related to pregnancy, you can start your leave then. Men are entitled to two weeks statutory paid paternity leave, in addition to annual holiday.

In the past, maternity leave and those delightful and terrifying early months at home with a new baby have been a mother's domain. But now new parents may get shared parental leave (SPL) and statutory shared parental pay (SSPP) if they're having a baby or adopting, although there's a set of criteria to meet first before claiming. A couple can share up to 50 weeks, 37 of which are paid. You might want to take it all in one go but it can be split up into blocks. The rules are complex – designed to put you to sleep (all that sleep that you will definitely need to catch up on).

Don't forget that pregnant women and the mothers of infants less than a year old are entitled to free NHS dentist care as well as free prescriptions in England. (Prescriptions are free for everyone in Scotland, Wales and Northern Ireland.)

CLAIM CHILD BENEFIT

He or she arrives! Such a lovely little creature and there is a big smile on everyone's face except perhaps the babe's! You have to register your baby, of course, and at the same time claim child benefit. Now, this is important. Until recently child benefit was paid to every parent – usually the mother – but, in 2013, the Government introduced a means-test – in other words, you only get it if your income is below a certain amount. Don't worry, it's not like the awful means-tests on income and capital that affect universal credit or tax credits or income support or housing benefit. It is a fairly genteel means-test on the best-off households – about one in eight, representing the ones with the highest incomes. At least that's the theory but it is – inevitably – more complex than that.

Like all means-tests it is complicated and puts many people off claiming it who should. So, here is my advice: no matter how much or little you earn, CLAIM YOUR CHILD BENEFIT. No ifs or buts. CLAIM IT. If I was allowed bigger type – oh, I am? Can I have colour or Day-Glo? No? OK then:

CLAIM CHILD BENEFIT

First, and most importantly (that's why it is first!), it is tax-free income. £21.80 a week for the first child and £14.45 for each child that follows. So, for three children it is more than £2600 a year tax-free. And it goes to the mother. Another big tick. That's the legacy of post-war politician Barbara Castle who died in 2002. Child benefit for every child paid to the mother was her, ahem, baby. She also made it illegal not to wear a seat-belt. So, she saved and improved millions of lives.

If you can only dream of having an annual income above £50,000 then you need not worry about the means-test. It is weird, complex and unfair, and only kicks in where the parent or their partner (who may or may not be the child's parent) has an income over £50,000 a year. So, if you both earn under £50,000 (in fact, for technical reasons if it is below £50,100) a year, you could just skip to page 14. BUT before you do, remember to come back here and read it just in case you or your partner, including a brand-new rich one, goes above that amount and the tax kicks in. The rules are widely seen as weird and unfair. So, the complex rules described next and in the child benefit rules box may be different or may not apply at all at some point in the future.

If either of you has an income above £50,000, child benefit is still paid to the mother, but the person with the higher income starts paying a special tax to give some of it back to the government. At £60,000 or more, the amount they pay back equals the child benefit. And it is income not just earnings. Also, there is a funny way of working out income – for example, you add on money for things like a company car and take off what you pay into a pension. I can explain the rules if you want. Yes? OK – see the box.

Child benefit rules

NB The government may change these rules in the future.

If your annual income is £50,000 or less AND your partner's annual income is less than £50,000, then ignore this box. If either of you has an income over £50,000 it applies. (Actually, the way the arithmetic works, you can each have an income of £50,099 without the charge applying, but I'm trying to keep things simple.)

A partner is defined as the person you live with as a couple. They may or may not be the parent of your children. The income of the children's other biological parent is irrelevant if they do not live with you as a partner.

The government counts what it calls 'adjusted net income'. So, how do you calculate this? It is your actual taxable income from a job (including any furlough payments during Covid) + self-employment profits + rents + taxable savings interest (not interest on an ISA and up to £500 a year elsewhere) + pensions (including state pension) and a few other state benefits. It also includes coronavirus grants from the Self-Employment Income Support Scheme (SEISS).

You can deduct payments to charity through Gift Aid and payments into a pension scheme. But then you must ADD ON the value of benefits from your employer, such as a company car. So even if your actual annual salary is below £50,000, a company car can push it over the limit.

What happens when your income exceeds £50,099? You are liable to high income child benefit charge. If income exceeds £60,000, then the charge is equal to the child benefit. In other words, you can still get child benefit but the partner with the higher income pays extra tax equal to it. If income is between £50,100 and £60,000, then some of your child benefit is taxed away. If your income is halfway between, then the tax equals half your child benefit. It's a sliding scale.

The **gov.uk** website does the sums at **gov.uk/child-benefit-tax-calculator** so you can see how it affects you.

And remember, it is a tax on the partner with the income above £50,000. If you both have that, then it is paid by the higher-paid person. And it does not matter if they are the child's parent or not.

But here is the reason why you should claim child benefit even if you are already well paid enough to have it all taken away by tax:

Every week that you are entitled to child benefit for a child under 12 (it used to be under 16) you will get a National Insurance credit towards your state pension. That is very valuable. If you claim child benefit – even if you then give it up or it is all taken away by tax as a better-off person – you will still get this credit. If you don't claim it, you won't get this credit. So, by not claiming it now – flouncing out saying, huh, what's £2600 a year tax-free to me darling! – you will be a lot poorer when you begin to wear out a bit and need money without working for it. So, have I mentioned, it is very important to:

CLAIM CHILD BENEFIT

OTHER BENEFITS

When the babe is born it may mean you are entitled to other benefits like universal credit, which is paid whether you are in work or not. Or a reduction in your council tax. Because a child – or an extra one – does normally boost the amount you get or mean you can get something that you couldn't before. The extra money for a child on universal credit is £244.58 (2022/23) a month. However, if you already have two children, you will not get any more because of the two-child rule. If you already have two children, a child born now (or 6 April 2017 or later) will not get you more money. Only the first two count. There are exceptions for twins or a child born as a result of rape, but in almost all cases the government's attitude is that three can live as cheaply as two for children whose parents are on universal credit. And if you have another, then four will have to live as cheaply as two. The only other countries in the world to have had such a policy in this century are the Communist states of Vietnam and China, which has recently become a three-child policy!

This two-child rule also applies to people who have not moved to universal credit and are still on child tax credits or housing benefit, which helps pay for rent. It will also probably apply if you are getting a reduction in your council tax because of your low income and you live in England. That will depend on where you live as councils make their own rules. It does not apply in Scotland or Wales to council tax reduction. In Northern Ireland, there is no council tax but it does not apply to the housing benefit and rate relief you get to help pay your rates or to rate rebate. Now you have an extra member of the family, it is important to check your entitlement to these means-tested benefits. You can do that online at **entitledto.co.uk**.

JUNIOR ISAS

Now, you have a babe in arms and you worry that it will need money when it gets older. You are not alone in this and there is a special way to save up for today's infants. It is called a Junior ISA or JISA. And like all other ISAs (there are five of them and they are all scattered through these pages), it comes with a choice – save or invest?

There is a BIG difference:

- If you SAVE, the money remains yours (or in fact the babe's).
- If you INVEST, then you give the money to someone else to make it grow.

Both are good and there are pros and cons to each. If you really can't decide, you can have one of each for a child – one in cash, the other invested. There is more on investing in general and the choices you make about that on page 195.

Whatever sort of JISA you choose you can put anything up to £9000 a year into it – and when I say 'you', I mean you, your partner if you have one, your parents, those friends down the road and that second cousin in Australia. Anyone can contribute to a child's JISA. But the total going in during the tax year must not exceed £9000 and if, by mistake, it does, then the extra is held by the government in a separate trust account for the child. Best not to let that happen.

Savings JISA

Is a JISA better than, say, an ordinary savings account? The rates paid even on the best JISAs are generally lower than those paid on the best children's savings accounts. The best savings JISA currently pays 3.1%. But the best children's savings account freed of the ISA invisibility cloak pays 3.5%, though they come with some restrictions. On a £3000 balance the best non-ISA will return your child £12 more this year than a JISA. These rates will have changed by the time you read this, but the principle will remain the same.

The main advantage that you will see widely quoted is that the interest earned in a JISA is tax-free. That does not matter because everyone – including the baby – gets a personal tax-free allowance and will not pay any tax until their income reaches at least £13,570 a year. Perhaps more in the future. Most babies have incomes below that! A savings account would have to be worth more than a third of a million pounds to generate that kind of money.

However, there is a potential tax trap. Money in a child's savings account put in by a parent can be taxed as if it was the parent's, so tax may be due. A JISA avoids that complication but there are other ways to avoid it.

Dodging the tax trap

If the child's savings account earns more than £100 interest in the year on money put in by a parent – so probably has £3000 in it – then all the interest counts as the parent's. That uses up part of their own savings allowance of £1000 a year (£500 if they pay higher rate tax and zero if they pay the 45% top rate of tax). Once that allowance is gone, then tax might be due. However, each parent has their own allowance and interest earned on money put in by grandparents or anyone else is not taxable. So it should be possible to remove this risk unless both parents have considerable savings themselves.

Right, after considering the above, you've made the decision to go with a JISA savings account. What can you expect?

Let us suppose the best rate stays at 3.1% (it won't, my rubber has gone right through the paper changing that one) and that you, granny and granddad put in £100 a month between you. By the time Slade is 18, they will have around £30,000 in their JISA, which, if inflation averages 5%, would be worth the same as £12,000 today. That is a good chunk of money for a round-the-world trip, a car, or even help towards a house deposit. Almost all of that is money you have put in. Even if you put in just £10 a month, then it will be just under £3000 for them at 18. By then enough for a really top party!

Stocks and shares JISA

The name is wrong of course. Stocks are the same as shares and your money doesn't have to be invested in shares (or stocks) at all. It can be in something safer, such as bonds or other stuff (we'll do more on investments later on page 195).

If we do not know what the rate paid on cash will be or what inflation will be, then we certainly do not know what the return on investments will be. We just don't. And anyone who says they do is lying – possibly to themselves, in which case they are telling you the truth as they see it, or possibly to you because they know they cannot predict the future but somehow they manage to make a living pretending they can.

There is one pretty firm rule: in the long-term, money invested in the stock market will outperform cash. But no-one knows how long 'long-term' is. Some may say as little as 5 years. Others 7 or 10 or 15. Most will agree that 20 is long-term. Ah, you think (and I have heard experienced financial advisers say it), a JISA lasts 18 years so that is surely long-term. Wrong! Simply wrong!! Only a fraction of the money is invested for 18 years. The average time invested is just nine years. Some is only invested for a year. So is that long-term? It's a tough one. But hey, you're a parent. Tough decisions come with the job. Only you can decide what is best for your child.

Check annual charges

If you give your money to someone else it may grow or it may shrink, and that person will want a cut for their part in making it grow or shrink (they tend to charge you either way). So, investing will come with charges that eat away at your JISA.

In the past, funds that were invested for children have had massive charges taken off them. You may remember child trust funds were invented by Gordon Brown and given to everyone born from 1 September 2002 to 2 January 2011. These were kickstarted with a £250 or a £500 gift from the state and they typically had 1.5% a year taken off them in charges every single year. In other words, the organisation investing them snaffled 1.5% of the total value of the fund (including what you put in) every year. A kind of mini-wealth tax. Why, I used to ask them, did they enjoy taking money off children? They muttered about small amounts, fixed costs and, mutter mutter mutter, I don't think that's a very fair question … which of course it was.

If you have a child born in that magic free-money time, then see page 35 in Chapter 3 for the £1000 windfall awaiting new 18-year-olds and how you or the 18-year-old can get hold of it.

The good news is that charges for investing have come down, though one of the biggest providers still charges 1.5%, taking as much as it can get away with from children. Others will still take a percentage every single year and even the typical 1% charge on a JISA will eat away at the growth. Sadly, most of those who talk about the long-term growth of investments often forget to include – or should I say deduct – the charges in their examples. Making them meaningless at best and deceitful at worst.

The past is no guide to the future, but if someone had put £100 a month into a stock market child trust fund and then a JISA 18 years ago, with growth and charges on a typical fund it would now be worth £34,666. That is a return of 6.7% after charges, which is pretty good. You would have put in £21,600 of that over the years, but it is still quite a sum to start your adult life with. And at only 18! I can hear parents feeling very uncomfortable about that!

What about that much-lauded tax-free status?

Well, it is just as pointless on an invested JISA as on a cash one. No income tax would be due on the dividends unless they exceeded £14,570 a year, which is highly unlikely. And it is very unlikely that capital gains tax would be due when it was cashed in. Except, of course, where wealthy parents have put in thousands a year or for those children who have large other incomes from work, self-employment, YouTubing or investments on which tax is already due. A tiny, tiny minority. And they have enough money to afford an accountant or a lawyer to advise them, not a £16.99 book.

Here is the best thing – and the worst thing – about any JISA. The child cannot get their hands on it until they are no longer a child. But on their 18th birthday, the whole lot becomes theirs to spend or squander as they see fit. Whether it is worth a crate of beer or a car or a house it is theirs. Get used to it. That cute little farting bundle of cuddliness (no, not your partner) will one day be an adult. And turn to Chapter 4.

Remember

- Up to £9000 in total per year can be put in a JISA and anyone can contribute.
- You must choose cash or investment – but a child can have one cash and one investment JISA.
- A cash ISA may not be as good as a regular child's savings account.
- For an investment JISA, keep the charges low and read the investment section first on page 195.
- At 18, everything in the JISA belongs to the new adult to do what they like with.

PENSION AT ONE-YEAR-OLD

If you want to put money away that your child cannot touch at 18, then you can start a secret account for them and you will decide when you give it to them. That may seem a bit mean, but some people think that 18 is far too young to be entrusted with what could be a large amount of money. This account wouldn't have any tax exemption and you may well end up paying tax on interest or dividends or, with investments, on the capital growth when you finally do hand it over at 21 or 25 or 30.

One way to get tax relief on the amount you put in and keep it tax-free while it grows is to start a pension for the child. Now, don't laugh. They will not be able to get their hands on it until their late fifties and surely by then, they will be responsible enough to handle it.

You can open the pension fund and put in up to £2880 a year. The kind old Treasury will boost that with another 25% or up to £720 a year. It is like taking money from a baby – except you are giving it to a baby! That fund will grow tax-free for the baby's life and at some time in their late fifties, they will be able to either cash it in or leave it until they retire.

This might seem a bit niche or daft or just plain unbelievable, but it can be done. The tax relief is given at the same rate in Scotland even though tax rates are different there. More on that little quirkiness on page 83 in Chapter 4. Be aware too that tax relief on pension contributions is controversial, very expensive and may change in the future. Long before baby Slade becomes a pensioner.

Remember

- Yes, you really can start a pension for a baby.
- You can put in up to £2880 a year and that is boosted by up to £720 (25% of what you put in) by the Treasury.
- It's an investment, so read the investment section on page 195.
- Baby cannot take it out until they are in their late fifties.
- Rules may change in the future.
- Is there anything else we can give to our young children, apart from money? Well, the gift of knowledge. Turn the page for my tips on these vital lessons.

CHILDHOOD 1–11

CHAPTER 2

Your children may seem young, but the way you deal with money at this age will affect your children for the rest of their lives. So do it well! You've got used to the costs of having a child by now. This chapter will help you make sure you get all the help with those costs that is there. But first ...

FINANCIAL EDUCATION

We teach children how to cross the road and brush their teeth as a matter of course. And it seems lessons on finance can't come soon enough if a response to one of our *Money Box* programmes is anything to go by. One woman explained the jam jar system she used for her daughter. When she was given money, the child had a choice of three jars in which to save, spend or share it. Through the glass sides she could watch the amount grow – or diminish if she chose to splash out. A teacher of three- to five-year-olds established a shop and gave her charges spending power and the scenario that they had a baby to care for. If children chose a packet of sweets they soon discovered they couldn't afford the very necessary nappies. It was a sterling start to teaching children how to prioritise need over want at the start of what's inevitably going to be a life-long lucre relationship.

It is hard to be against financial education. It seems a no-brainer. Teach kids about money at school and they will cope better with it as they become adults. But I have to tell you it is not the whole answer. Not at all. **The most important thing you can give your children is the ability to read and do sums.** Too many of them leave school not very literate and functionally innumerate. But money is just about adding and subtracting – and that is basically just counting in two directions. So make sure they can do that. We'll come on to percentages later because a lot of adults – dare I say a lot of journalists and, even, whisper it, some financial journalists – struggle with them.

Money is like sex. No, don't misunderstand me! Children should be slowly learning the essentials of it, at whatever pace and whatever way you think is – to use the current jargon – age-appropriate. Between the two magic ages of 1 and 11, there is an opportunity to start this learning about money.

Research shows that kids learn from what their parents do. So, your attitude to money – managing it, borrowing it, earning it, squandering it – will rub off on the kids, especially once they are seven or eight. As a Cambridge University study put it, slightly more formally than I would, most young children have grasped all the main aspects of how money works and formed what it called 'core behaviours, which they will take into adulthood and which will affect financial decisions they make during the rest of their lives'.

So, set a good example. And let them learn from life what earning money, buying things, paying tax, rent and bills are all about. The very worst thing to do is to hide it from them so they know nothing about it when they first come across it. There, I told you it was like sex! There's a thirst for knowledge about money issues among young people and an easy familiarity with it will help them deal with the financial complexities ahead.

Pocket money – cash or card?

Pocket money is a good way to start. Now, us oldies – and I include you in that if you are a parent – probably think of pocket money being given in £1 coins. And I am still a great fan of that – though when I was young it was a sixpence or a shilling! Of course, you may argue – it's a book, I can't hear you! but do go on – that the future for today's children is not cash. And that is true. And I am a great fan of giving them a card they can use as cash. But there is something simple, visceral almost, in having cash that you can count out and give change from and which really helps with those arithmetic skills. A piece of plastic does not do that. Imagine Monopoly without the banknotes! Come to that, playing Monopoly is very good training in money and financial life. Not just the mental arithmetic but the sheer unfairness of it all.

Let us start with coins. I would actually keep a little stash of coins just for teaching. Then you know you've got pennies, 2ps, fives, 10ps, twenties, 50ps and £1 and £2 coins. Eight different coins. So what do those different coins mean? It can be fun counting them out and stacking up pennies to equal a 10p piece and ten 10ps to equal a pound. You could even show them that a 1p weighs half a 2p and a 5p half a 10p. How? Well with a kitchen scale and little piles of them. And it shouldn't matter whether they are coins of Elizabeth II or Charles III.

Coins and notes are the basis of money, even though most of it now is on a plastic card. Visualising money as notes and coins helps kids to understand that when it's gone, it's gone. And that is why survey after survey finds that millions of people still value cash and like using cash. So, teaching cash to kids is a vital life skill – even as we come to the end of the first quarter of the twenty-first century.

However, a plastic card does help young people deal with money as adults do – though, of course, more and more of their money will be on their phone and by the time a ten-year-old is an adult, even plastic cards may be found mainly in a museum of currency.

So, open an account for your child round about the end of this era at 10 or 11. There are firms that will let the child use the card but also tell you, the parent, what they do with it. Don't look on this as spying ... in fact, yes, do look on this as spying because that is what it is! If a child is not allowed to go out by themselves, why should they have access to money to spend without some adult supervision?

Teaching how to budget

Some people give pocket money monthly, or even six-monthly, to help children get a feel for budgeting. And every parent has to decide if pocket money is an allowance or a wage – given as long as they do certain duties like feeding the hamster or emptying the dishwasher – and how that might change over time. There are plenty of other ways to interest young people when it comes to managing domestic finances. I heard one father say he gave his 11-year-old responsibility for booking the family holiday! He was happy to report the break was a success and that now holiday planning is always handed over to the younger generation. I bet he kept a careful eye on it all!

While it may be natural to shield children from any monetary crisis hitting the household, my view is that sharing financial concerns with your children is a great way of teaching real-life lessons about money. And you never know, a fresh young brain may even suggest a good solution. Children can source less expensive brands of their favourite food during a supermarket shop, for example, or choose the way they would prefer to make economies from a set of options.

Ironically, the recent staggering rises in the price of electricity and gas are an ideal opportunity to remind kids to turn off lights, switch off chargers that are not being used and, when they are old enough, only put enough water in the kettle for the cup or pot of tea they are making. They can also be encouraged to have shallower baths and shorter showers. They really do all cost money now.

I was not a fan of smart meters but the one big advantage they do have is the in-home display (IHD), which can be used to teach kids what costs a lot of energy and what costs less. Let them see the numbers mount up when the kettle or washing machine is on. One excellent lesson for us all is that generally anything that uses electricity to heat something up – whether it is water, an iron or the house – is expensive. And although keeping the TV on standby and the Wi-Fi on 24/7 is convenient, turning it off every night will save money in the long run. And that smart meter in-home display may show you how much. And even if it is just pence a day, multiply it by 30 and that comes off your monthly bill. What things cost is the cornerstone of teaching money.

More direct ways to help them understand money can be to let them pay! If you're going out on a trip, add up the cost of the things you will need – bus fares, snacks, etc.. Then put that cash in a separate purse and put them in charge of paying and getting change. If they want crisps and an ice cream, you can explain that then there won't be enough to get home on the bus and you'll have to walk.

The other side of money is of course income. Mum, where does money come from? It's a philosophical question many adults struggle to answer! Not least because the truth is governments just make it up. But don't get me started on that! Again, in an age-appropriate manner, explain about earning money, benefits (if you think you don't get benefits, then remember almost every parent gets child benefit and all grannies over 66 get a pension), interest, dividends, rent and so on. Just to know that money isn't something magic, or indeed something that you are always short of, but is simply a fact of life. And just as their pocket money is finite and never quite enough, so it is with the rest of us.

Spending money is one thing but saving it to buy something special or just to possess it is another. I prefer using a jar to a piggy bank because you can see the money and watch it pile up as you put a certain amount into it each week. Also, piggy banks cost money and then have to be smashed, which is a very hefty negative rate of interest!

Managing money – in and out – is the best life lesson and you are never too young to start. And because money is actually nice to have and to spend, knowing about it can make learning addition, subtraction, multiplying and dividing fun. The government is trying to boost numeracy among schoolchildren and you as parents can play your part through money, just as you boost literacy by reading to them and getting them to read to you.

Remember

- Reading and basic arithmetic are essential to managing money.
- Children learn their habits from you, so manage your money in the way you want them to.

- Don't hide money problems from them.
- Coins, as well as a simple account with a plastic card, can help them learn about money.
- Involve them in money decisions when you can.

FREE SCHOOL MEALS

Getting your child fed at school is a very big saving. The rules are slightly different in different parts of the UK.

In England, a child in year 2 or below is given a free school lunch whatever the income of their parent. In Scotland, that extends up to year 5.

Older children will get free school lunches and sometimes breakfast or milk and fruit if their parent is on a means-tested benefit, such as child tax credit, income support, income-based jobseeker's allowance or employment and support allowance. For parents on universal credit, the rules are more complicated as you also must have a household income of less than £7400 a year. Benefits do not count towards that total and it is counted after tax and National Insurance contributions. That income test was introduced for new claims – including a claim for an extra child – from 1 April 2018.

There are different, and generally better, criteria in the rest of the UK. You claim through your local authority. Children who get free meals should not be discriminated against and no other children or parents should know if they get their meals free or not. Though, of course, they may not like the school meals as much as a lunchbox you make. But this is another good opportunity to talk to them about money and how it works.

CHILDCARE COSTS

The UK has some of the most expensive childcare in the world. The OECD (Organisation for Economic Co-operation and Development) is an international body that likes to draw up lists. And it found that the UK is third in the list of the most expensive countries for childcare. It costs 30 per cent of the average wage to have a child looked after while you work. That will come as no surprise to working parents; mothers particularly, as it is women who normally have to balance the cost of childcare against the income they might get by returning to work as their children grow up.

There is quite a lot of help available for working parents and a certain amount of childcare may be free. The rules seem to be designed to be complex and, of course, vary between England, Scotland, Wales and Northern Ireland. Most of the childcare and the help with it is provided through the local authority where you live, so ask it first about what you can get.

The UK government does have information about the rules in all four parts of the UK on its **gov.uk** website Try **childcarechoices.gov.uk** and, even better perhaps, is the childcare calculator **gov.uk/childcare-calculator**.

Universal credit

If you are on universal credit (see page 102), you can get up to 85 per cent of your childcare costs paid in addition to your benefit. There are numerous rules. They include that the child must be under 16 and, of course, you must be working. The childcare provider must be registered, though the precise rules for that vary between England, Scotland, Wales and Northern Ireland. There is a maximum amount that will be paid, which is £646.35 a month for one child and £1108.04 for two or more children. You get the same amount whether you have two children or ten because of the two-child rule (see page 14 in Chapter 1 for more on that). At the moment, you have to pay for the childcare in advance, though that is subject to a legal challenge. If that is difficult or impossible, talk to your work coach.

Working tax credit

Fewer and fewer people are still on working tax credits. It does come with help for childcare, but it may be better to move to universal credit. It is a fiendish calculation but you can do it at **benefits-calculator.turn2us.org.uk**.

England

All working parents can get up to 15 hours of free childcare a week for three- and four-year-olds for 38 weeks of the year. It ends when the child starts school. You can get another 15 hours, making 30 in all, if you are a working single parent or in a couple where you both work at least 16 hours a week and, of course, you must get the minimum wage for your age. You are not eligible if you, or either of you, earns more than £100,000 a year. Childcare providers will tell you more and, for a price, sell you more hours if you need them. Self-employed people can qualify too and there are, again, complications and exceptions.

If your child is two, then you can get similar help but only if you are on one of the seven means-tested benefits (see page 7 for the list). For most people now that will mean getting universal credit. With that, you also have to have a household income of £15,400 a year or less after tax. You do not count benefit payments in that total. If you are on one of the older means-tested benefits, you may also qualify. They include income support, means-tested jobseeker's allowance or employment and support allowance. If you still get child tax credits and your household income is no more than £16,190 a year (before tax), you can qualify. People over 66 who get the guaranteed element of pension credit can also qualify.

Scotland

Funded early learning and childcare in Scotland has similar age, work and benefits rules to the schemes in England. But Scotland is steadily improving its welfare provision and it is important to check what is currently available with your local council and on the mygov.scot website.

Wales

Flying Start applies in some parts of Wales and offers free childcare for two- and three-year-olds. It is two-and-a-half hours a day for 39 weeks. The Childcare Offer for Wales is 30 hours of early education and childcare for children aged three or four for up to 48 weeks a year for almost all working parents throughout the country. The conditions are similar to those in England but it lasts for an extra 10 weeks of the year, so covers school holidays. Check what is available in your area at **childcareinformation.wales**.

Northern Ireland

There is no free childcare as such in Northern Ireland, but you may be able to get your child a place in free education for the year before they start at primary school. You must apply online on the Education Authority website.

UK wide

There is also a scheme called tax-free childcare, which simply means that the government pays £2 of every £10 of the cost up to a limit of £500 payment every three months – which is £2000 a year towards your fees for each child under the age of 12. To get that help, you need to set up an online account and so does the childcare provider. The latest figures show six out of ten parents who could get this subsidy do not! Make sure you get yours. You can get this as well as other free childcare. The work and income limits are the same but limits for a child with disabilities may be higher. You cannot get tax-free childcare and get extra universal credit or child tax credits to pay for the care. Make sure you check which would be best for you at the **gov.uk/childcare-calculator**.

In all cases, the childcare provider must be registered. Tax-free childcare is available throughout the UK.

Relatives and childcare

If your child is looked after by a relative, such as a grandparent or cousin, you cannot claim money under any of the schemes for help with childcare unless they are also a registered childminder or carer. However, if a relative who is under state pension age looks after your children so you can work, they may be entitled to claim credits towards their National Insurance record. The child must be under 12 and you must get child benefit for them. Normally, you could claim National Insurance credits. But if you work and pay National Insurance contributions for the whole year, then you don't need these credits and they can be passed to a relative who cares for your children so you can work.

These credits are called Class 3 and count towards qualifying for the state pension. Normally you need 35 years to get a full one, but some people even with 35 years will find their pension is higher if they get these credits now.

To qualify, the relative must provide care every week during the tax year. The rules are very lax. As long as they look after your child for some time during every week, that is sufficient. It can be as little as meeting them after school in term time one or two days a week and then in the holidays taking them out or giving them lunch at home.

Grandparents under state pension age are the most likely people to benefit from these credits. But any relative can and the definition of that is very broad – siblings, aunts, uncles and their spouses or partners – even former partners! – all count. Half- and adopted relatives are also included. However, for any year only one person can get the credits.

They can claim from 31 October for the previous tax year – so claim in October 2023 for the tax year 2022/23. And if they fulfilled the conditions, they can claim back four more years.

You get the claim form at **gov.uk** – search 'specified adult childcare'. You and the relative have to claim together.

If you do care for the children of relatives, then the organisation Kinship Carers has lots of useful information **kinship.org.uk**.

Remember

- Childcare is more expensive in the UK than in almost any other developed country. So claim what you can towards the cost as it will help you get back to work. The rules can seem complex and daunting. Try the government's childcare choices and childcare calculator – they work anywhere in the UK. And if your mum or another relative under pension age helps you, then make sure they claim the free National Insurance contributions if they need them.

CHAPTER 3

TEENS 12–18

Hey, 12–18s, this is the first chapter aimed at you, not your parents. Though please let them read it too. Now you can start to manage your money by yourself. It covers some basics but some other bits are in the next couple of chapters. So, feel really grown up and, like when you are on a night out, pretend you are 18–23 and read that chapter too!

CHILD TRUST FUND

You are a lucky generation of people if you were born between 1 September 2002 and 2 January 2011, inclusive (i.e. those aged 12–20 at the start of 2023). You have a special pot of money saved up for you in a child trust fund. It will probably be around £1000 and the moment you reach 18 it is yours. It could be more if kind people have added to it. It could be less if no-one has. Whatever it is, you can take it out and spend it. Sorry, all you young twenties born before that crucial date. And the just 12s and under who were born after 2 January 2011. You don't get £1000. Who said life was fair? Not me. In fact, it is lesson number one.

The child trust fund was a scheme established by the late lamented Chancellor Gordon Brown (I know he's not dead, but he did some good things). The idea was that every child had access to savings when they became an adult. To encourage parents, grandparents and friends to contribute to the tax-free fund, the government itself made several contributions, and these were doubled for low-income families, pushing the total to £1,000 in government contributions for a few. The first paydays to 18-year-olds came on 1 September 2020 and everyone who comes of age for the next decade will have an account with their name on it.

Sadly, many parents and many children and young adults are unaware of it. Indeed, some parents remained unaware even when it was launched or when their baby was born and never opened the child trust fund account for them. If they ignored the government's pleas to do so for a year, then an account was established in their child's name anyway by the Treasury. Even those who did open one may have lost the paperwork (yes, paperwork. They are that old) and personal identification numbers are long forgotten. There are fears that the money held in up to a third of the roughly six million accounts will go unclaimed by newly minted 18-year-olds. Parents, if you are reading this, use this moment to start the little ones on an adult life of expecting free money! 'Happy Birthday darling, let me help you find your one thousand pounds!' There are two ways of claiming their cash:

- **Visit the government's own website and access the money by creating a Gateway account.** That is not particularly user-friendly but it is useful to have a Government Gateway account and may one day be essential.
- **Use a charity called the Share Foundation findctf.sharefound.org, which will do it for free.** Apart from personal details that everyone has – name, address, date of birth – you will need your National Insurance number. Once you have access to your fund, you can take it out in cash or roll it over to an ISA. That stands for Individual Savings Account and the interest or dividends the money earns is tax-free. See ISA nonsense on page 122.

If you are one of the estimated 880,000 young people who need help from an adult because you do not have what is called 'mental capacity', then your parent or the person who cares for you should be able to access your fund quite easily. Until 2021 it was much more difficult but new rules have been promised and once they start, it should mean there is not a problem.

NATIONAL INSURANCE NUMBER

Another landmark moment comes about three months before you reach 16. You will be sent a National Insurance number. This is always two capital letters, six digits and then one capital letter, which is always A, B, C or D, such as SM398867D – I generated that at random, so if it's yours I apologise, but only you know that! This odd format was devised (for good reasons then) in the middle of the last century. If you are already 16 or older and have not got one, then that is probably because your mum did not claim child benefit for you. You should contact His Majesty's Revenue

& Customs (HMRC) on 0300 200 3500. Make a cup of tea and load some sounds as you may be hanging on for a while. Welcome to the adult world of dealing with money!! HMRC will not tell you the number but will post it to you. It could take eight weeks and you will probably have to send in documents to prove who you are.

You will need this number to get a job (you can be employed without one, as long as you are applying for it), open a bank account, invest, claim benefits, open your personal tax account and all sorts of other things. It is not officially an identity number, but it is a number and does identify you and is now widely used with your date of birth to do just that. Write it down somewhere safe. It is useful to memorise it just in case. Having said that, I still can't remember mine!

YOUR FIRST JOB

Once you are 16, you can be employed to do work for money and can start doing all those interesting things like paying tax! In other words, you earn an extra £50 and the government snaffles a chunk of it before you see it. The full horrors – sorry, I mean 'details' – of taxes on wages are in Chapter 4 on page 81.

In summary, if you earn more than £242 in a week you will pay two taxes on the money over that amount:

- Income tax takes 20% of what you earn above that amount.
- National Insurance is another tax of 12% of everything you earn above £242 a week.

Add them up – that is 32% of what you earn. Nearly a third of everything you earn above £242 a week is snaffled by the government. So, if you earn £254 that is £12 above £242 and that is taxed, so nearly £4 disappears back to the Chancellor. Welcome to the real world. Even more can disappear as you earn more, but we'll leave it for now. In Scotland, there is a starter rate of 19% for what you earn from £242 to £283 a week, when it switches to the basic rate of 20%. From April 2023, there may be changes in rates and thresholds in Scotland.

Minimum wage

By law, everyone is paid a minimum amount per hour. The amount changes each April and depends on your age. The rate for people aged 23 or more is called the National Living Wage, but that does not mean anyone can live on it! It was a political renaming by the Chancellor in 2015.

Official legal minimum wages per hour (these change every April)

	Minimum wage per hour as of 1 April 2022
23 and over (called National Living Wage)	£9.50
21 to 22	£9.18
18 to 20	£6.83
Under 18	£4.81
Apprentice	£4.81

A charity called the Living Wage Foundation publishes what it calls the Real Living Wage each Autumn with one rate for London and another for the rest of the UK. It is currently £11.95 an hour in London and £10.90 everywhere else. That, it reckons, is the minimum people need to live on if they work 37½ hours a week. Many firms have committed to paying it, but it is not the official rate.

SIDE HUSTLES

If you want extra money, then a side hustle can be a good way to earn some. Writing, managing social media accounts for a local small business, buying clothes at a bargain price and reselling them on eBay or Depop, dog walking, baby-sitting, driving – the possibilities are as endless as your imagination and abilities.

Beware adverts offering you money for work at home or anything that demands money up front from you, especially ones you find on social media – assume they are scams (see page 127 on Fraud and page 45 on Social media). Never agree to let someone pass money through your account for a small fee. That is always illegal money being moved and you become a money mule and commit a crime by doing it. You could find yourself blocked from a bank account for years and that would prevent you getting a student loan and may stop you getting benefits or even a job. You might go to jail.

If you do have a side hustle, you can make £1000 a year without reporting it. But once your turnover – the total of your sales, not your profit – exceeds that, then you do have to tell the taxman, aka His Majesty's Revenue & Customs (HMRC), and tax may be due.

BANK ACCOUNTS

At 16 you can open a bank or building society account even without permission from your mum or dad. Money you earn or are given can be paid in and you can have a card – called a debit card – to spend the money in your account online or take out cash. Very grown up. But you also must be very grown up yourself about spending online. There are crooks out there that will try to steal your money while seeming to be very friendly. You wouldn't hand money to a stranger on the street who promised to sell you something. Be just as suspicious online. Read about Social media on page 45 and Fraud on page 127.

STUDENT LOANS

If you are in education after the age of 18 you may be able to get grants – sometimes call bursaries – to help pay for your expenses and other costs. Ask at the college where you want to go. They will be very different in different parts of the UK.

If you go to university, as around half of 18–21 years olds do, the arrangements are much more complicated. But let me say at the start they all involve what is called a 'student loan'. And you will see some eye-watering figures for how much you will owe after three years study – and it is of course even more humungous if you do medicine or architecture, where the courses last more than three years. What do I mean by eye-watering? £65,000. Or more. Yes, really. That is what you could owe by the time you put on that mortar board and gown. But write this on your hand and read it every hour – **THIS IS NOT A LOAN**. At least, not in the normal sense of the word.

OK, you borrow the money and it is paid back by you. But it is not like a commercial loan. **For those living in England and starting uni in 2023, the new rules are:**

- If your salary is below £25,000, you do not pay back a penny.
- Once your salary exceeds that amount, you are charged an extra 9% tax on the excess along with income tax etc.
- Interest is added to the loan at the current rate of inflation measured by the Retail Prices Index (RPI). That is currently over 12% and this rule may be changed.
- After 40 years, the loan is written off.

If you first went to uni in 2022 or right back to 2012, the threshold where you start paying back is £27,295, the tax is the same, interest is RPI or RPI plus up to 3% in some cases, and the write-off happens after 30 years, not 40. In Scotland, the threshold is £25,000, the tax is the same, and the write-off 30 years. Scottish debt is much less because Scottish students at Scottish universities do not pay tuition fees.

Although it is called a loan, the repayments go up and down with your pay and at average pay levels, can be quite modest.

Someone with an income of £30,000 a year will pay 9% on £5000 or £450 per year, which is just £37.50 a month. It will automatically be taken from their monthly pay along with income tax and National Insurance contributions.

If you lose your job, your pay falls to £25,000 or less or you take time off work, for example due to illness or to have a baby, then no repayments are made. And for about four out of ten new graduates, the loan will be written off before they have paid it all back. It would be much simpler if the government was honest and straightforward and called the 9% extra tax just that – a graduate tax.

A student loan does not affect your credit score, so it won't affect whether you can get a mortgage or a personal loan. Though it will mean you have less spare income and that may affect how much you can borrow.

Sharia loans

Some Muslim students are reluctant or unwilling to take out a student loan because interest is charged on it. That is against Islamic law. Many Muslim students try to pay for themselves without a loan – working long hours in a job in some cases and damaging their ability to study and take part in university life. Others object to paying the interest, but accept it and feel guilty the whole time.

This problem only arose after the loan started to attract interest in 2012. In 2013, the government promised to provide an alternative. Ten years on, it still has not done so, even though Islamic scholars have designed a student loan that would be identical financially but would conform to Sharia law. The solution, drawn up in 2014, would provide the loans from a ring-fenced fund for those who took part. Like other students, they would pay back more than they took out. Although that extra money would be identical in amount, it would not be interest and would remain in the fund to provide bursaries and grants for other students who could not otherwise afford a university education. This mutual benefit makes it acceptable to Muslims. The government has said it intends to introduce Sharia student loans in 2025. If it does, they will be open to any student who wants one.

Remember

- Student loans change for new students from September 2023.
- Student loans are not like other loans.
- If your income falls, repayment is suspended.
- After 40 years, the loan is written off.

SOCIAL MEDIA

Sorry, I don't want to sound like an OK Boomer, but social media is a dangerous place. I know it's fun, I spend hours on it myself, but there are some things I never do on it. Here's why.

I once wrote a book that had a lot of golden rules. Some of them were golden and sparkly rules. And the most important had jewels on as well.

If I could do that here, this would be the diamond-encrusted platinum rule:

Never, ever, ever, ever take investment or financial advice from anyone on social media

OK, that's it. Follow that rule and you will not lose money in a get-rich-quick scheme, not be seduced by the compound interest tricks of teenagers, and never be fooled by the thieves that pretend their idea is supported by a celeb. No real-world celeb would ever endorse anything on such platforms. By which I mean, they would only endorse things if they knew nothing about money and were paid to promote it. That's how influencers work. But no journalist or financial expert who knew anything about investment would do it. If you see one, it is a fraud.

YouTube, TikTok, Instagram, Snapchat, Twitter and, for you older readers, WhatsApp, Facebook, Telegram and

LinkedIn, to name but nine, are all haunted by denizens of the underworld. There are influencers on all those channels – many of whom have far less followers than I do! – who say they can give you advice about investments, schemes to make money easily and quickly, pay off debt, repair your credit score and so on. But I refer you to the rule above.

Social media might be a fun place, but it is also lawless. Despite attempts by the government – still wending their glacial way through Parliament after four years of discussion – it is almost impossible to regulate publishers who have no real physical place on Earth. They are everywhere and nowhere. And there is no silver lining. So you often cannot find out who is behind the advice or ideas you see.

If anyone promises you quick instant money, often called a 'moneyflip', it's a fraud. The story is that you send them money, it's invested on the foreign exchange or crypto markets, and when they rise you get your money back with a bit added. These are all frauds. All of them. Sometimes they are used by crooks to get you to launder the proceeds of their crimes. By doing that, you become what is called a money mule – see page 40 in Chapter 3 for more on that. The other problem with Insta is that thieves take over accounts, so you think it is your friend offering you these instant-wealth products.

So, the only safe rule is just don't do it. No-one ever lost money by ignoring get-rich-quick schemes.

WHEN TO TRUST SOCIAL MEDIA

What? You just said never etc. etc. I did. And it is still my advice. You won't lose any money by following that advice. But as with any rules, there are exceptions. A growing number of trained, qualified and regulated advisers do have their own channels and presence on social media. So, if you find one who is qualified and regulated and, of course, independent (see page 206 in Investing), then they can be trusted on social media as well as they can anywhere else. They won't give you personal individual regulated advice because that is not allowed. But they will give you useful information. One mortgage broker, who does a lot online, told *Money Box*, 'I do mortgages every day. Most people do them a few times in their life. So I can offer useful insights about the process, what to look for – and look out for.'

If you come across someone like this, then ignore their social media presence and check them out separately yourself. You can see if someone or their firm is regulated by the Financial Conduct Authority on its website **fca.org.uk** – search 'register'. But beware clones. The FCA also has pages listing crooked firms that pretend to be respectable, registered firms. This cloning can be very sophisticated, so check by searching 'clones' on the FCA website.

THE CRYPTO FACTOR

Bitcoin and cryptocurrencies are not investments. They are gambles. You gamble that the person selling them is honest. That the place you store them is real. And that when you want to cash them in, no-one will steal them on the way. Sure, you know someone who has made enough for a deposit on their first home. Or bought a brand-new car. Or at least you have heard of them through a friend. Or a friend's cousin. One major bank told me that one in five withdrawals to buy crypto assets was fraudulent. If you want to dip your toe into this exciting new world, make sure it is a toe you are happy to lose. Because the chances are you will. See page 133 in Fraud for more on crypto fraud.

CHAPTER 4

STARTING OUT 18–23

Whoopee. You're an adult. Amazing. You may not feel like one and your mum will still fuss over you but you are legally an adult. You can vote. You can borrow! Get a credit card!! But out there is the dangerous world of finance. If you are not careful, it can take advantage of you.

Before we come onto that though, turn back to child trust funds on page 35 in the last chapter because 18 is the age when you can unlock the £1000 that is waiting as a golden hello to adulthood. Don't ignore it.

BANKS – HOW THEY WORK

Let's be clear about one thing. Banks are not your friends. They can be very useful and in many ways they are essential, but they are there to make money. And unlike most other businesses, they don't do that by making something you want like a PS4 or a car. They make money out of money. People have railed against them for doing that for – well, for as long as people have railed. Aristotle started it. Money, he said (I paraphrase and he said it in Greek anyway), is simply a means of exchange. It lets me buy a coat now without having to wait for my goat to have kids so I can barter one of them for a new coat, probably when winter is over. But, he went on, money should not be used to make money. For example, someone who already has a coat uses some spare money to buy another and then he rents it out to someone with less money so they can keep warm. But he then demands two kids to repay the loan. People with money using it to take money from people who have less. That is roughly what Aristotle said about making money out of money more than three hundred years before Christ was born.

Making money out of money is what banks do – and have done for centuries – so get used to it. Of course, banks are very useful. Without banks to lend people money to buy a house, or start a business, or update that old tractor, the world would be a poorer place. On the other hand, they also lend money to firms to do things that damage the environment. Many think the world would be a better place without that.

Banks will always be helpful to you if they can make money out of you at little or no risk. As long as they can do that, then you will have a good relationship with them. You may even see them as *very* helpful. Without the bank, you could not have bought your car. You could not make instant payments when you want to buy a new dress. They keep your money safe and do all the pesky sums so you know, every nanosecond if you want to, just how much you have (or haven't) got. But if the balance of risk tips away from a clear profit, they will not help. Full stop. Always look at them in that light. They are your good friend – until they are not. And in passing, I might mention that they have been fined billions of pounds for rigging markets, mis-selling to customers, and not stopping money laundering. Always bear that in mind.

CURRENT ACCOUNTS

There are some things the banks do for nothing – or seem to. You probably do not pay a fee for your current account. If you do, then it is generally best to switch to a free one. More on that shortly. This is unusual. In most countries, customers pay for their current account. After all, the bank is providing a valuable service – keeping your money safe, doing all the sums, and letting you transfer it in a picosecond to someone else. Over the years, the banks have devised ways to make us pay for it (see the overdrafts section on page 57), but current accounts do not really make the banks any money. Which they hate.

Making regular payments

Your current account is where it all happens. Money in – wages, your aunt's birthday surprise (not as much as you hoped), benefits perhaps, your student loan. And, of course, money out – did I really spend £72.50 in that pub? There are three ways you can let a business take money out of your account without telling them every time.

Standing order

You make a standing order (SO), when you decide to pay a fixed amount on a fixed date to a named firm. These are not very popular now but you are completely in control of them.

Direct debit

A direct debit (DD) is different. You give the firm permission to take money out of your account. That permission is normally for it to take any amount at any time. Usually of course it is a regular amount every month to pay your electricity bill, mobile phone or credit card balance. Nowadays, most big firms can set one up over the phone or online and you do not have to sign anything. Direct debits come with a really important guarantee – called, yes, the Direct Debit Guarantee! Although the firm can take any amount it likes at any time it likes, it has to notify you of a change ten days before it happens. If a mistake is made, you are entitled to a full and immediate refund by your own bank. You can cancel a DD at any time immediately by telling your bank. These are important rights. All banks will let you see a list of your standing orders and direct debits, usually on the app.

Continuous payment authority

The third way you can let a company take money from you is one most people seem unaware of. It is used widely for online payments when you subscribe to something or agree a payment using your debit card, either online or on the phone. Whenever you hear 'what's the long number on your card' or you fill it in online, you are potentially giving the firm what is called a continuous payment authority (CPA) to take money out of your bank account. Like a direct debit, it can be any amount at any time. But unlike DDs and SOs, you will not normally see these listed when you log on to online banking.

These CPAs are so easy to give permission for that we often have them on our bank account without realising it. For example, you sign up for a free trial period of the game TraffleBoard. The free trial lasts for a month. Great – it's free and it might be fun. In fact, it is set in Dullsville, the music is from the nineties and you get fed up with all the adverts. So you stop playing it. What you didn't realise is that when you signed up you agreed to pay for it – £8.99 a month in advance forever. That happened when the firm took the details of your debit card. So, after the first free month £8.99 is snaffled from your bank account. And in June. And in July. And so on. Until you stop it.

Unlike DDs, these payments come with no guarantee. You cannot get a list of them from your bank, so you must – boring! – check your bank statement every month at least. **When you see a payment you do not recognise or understand, track it down and, if you don't want it, stop it (see How to stop an unwanted CPA in box below).**

These CPAs can also be taken from a credit card or PayPal. The same problems can arise and the same rights apply. You have the absolute right to stop them with your credit card provider or PayPal just by telling them to do so. And, yes, sorry but it does mean you have to check your credit card and PayPal statements too. Though with PayPal you should get a notice by email of when the payment is taken, which is a useful warning.

How to stop an unwanted CPA

Firms try to make it difficult. To cancel it, you may be told you have to call, or even write a letter. They hope you'll not bother. But CPAs now come with an absolute right to stop them just by telling your bank.

- **Step 1:** Email or phone or app them 'Stop making payments to Xnartiuvc. I withdraw my consent to any such payments from today.' Your bank must do it.
- **Step 2:** Send an email to Xnartiuvc saying the same thing – but the bank comes first because that will stop the payment. If the bank makes a payment after you have made that call or sent that message, the bank has to reimburse you for it. If there is no easy email for Xnartiuvc, look up the firm that runs it and send them an email. Worse comes to worst, write them a physical letter on paper and post it to their head office.
- **Step 3:** Once the payments stop, it will soon try to find you. Say you did not agree to it or, if you did, the wording was unclear and you will not pay. If it insists you have a contract until 2043, just refuse and wait for it to take you to court. It almost certainly won't and if it does, write to the court explaining that it broke Part 2 (Unfair terms) of the Consumer Rights Act 2015.

For more on rights like these, you should get a copy of Helen Dewdney's book *How to Complain* (2019). It does precisely what it says.

Interest: a simple guide

Forgive me if you know all about interest. But I have had to explain it to enough colleagues to know that even people interested in money do not. Especially that thing dubbed the eighth wonder of the world – **compound interest**.

Interest is simple. Interest of 1% means that if you have savings that pay 1% a year, then you get £1 of interest for every £100 you have saved. Percentage just means that much per hundred. If it pays 2.15%, then you would get £2.15 for every hundred pounds invested. Easy peasy.

If that interest was paid into your current account to give you an income, then after ten years you would have earned £21.50, your £100 would be intact in your savings account and still earning £2.15 every year.

But suppose the interest was saved in your savings account instead?

After year one, you wouldn't have £100 in there, but £102.15. So, in year two you would earn 2.15% on £102.15, not £100. That is £2.20. And that is kept in the account, so that at the end of year 3 you would have £106.59 and so on. At the end of year ten, you would have earned £23.70 not £21.50. OK, so what you say? A couple of quid?

But suppose you had earned more interest. Say you had £10,000 at the start and 4.5% each year.

Then after 20 years, instead of earning 20 x £450 = £9000 interest, you would have earned £14,117. And after 40 years, instead of earning £18,000 interest, it would have been £48,164. And 40 years is the time – in theory – that you have a pension investment.

So, the rules of compound interest on savings and investments are:

- It is always better than simple interest on savings or investments.
- The higher the interest rate and the longer the period, the better it is.

So, is it the eighth wonder of the world? Google that and you will find this attributed to Albert Einstein or John Rockefeller. But neither of them actually said or wrote it. People say they did because attributing it to a genius or the first billionaire makes it seem true. It was probably written by a Cleveland USA advertising copywriter in 1925 to persuade people to invest in a savings bond.

One thing is for sure, compound interest has a dark side. Because it applies equally to debt. It means that if a debt has an interest rate of 15%, you pay £15 a year in interest on every £100 borrowed. And if you do not pay that interest off, then after year one it is compounded. After five years, your debt has doubled. After eight years it has trebled. After ten years it has quadrupled. And after 20 years it is 16 times bigger! Yes. £100 borrowed becomes £1637 in 20 years. So this is how banks make their money. Getting you into debt at high rates and keeping you there. Or they did. Now there are strict rules about this that should make things better.

If you are not into Excel spreadsheets, skip this bit. If you are, you can work out your debt after compound interest with this formula:

D=B*(1+R)^Y

As you know ^ means to the power …

And here is what it stands for:

D (debt) = B (amount borrowed)
x (1 + R (interest rate)) ^ Y (the number of years)

Overdrafts

One business that always has a right to take money from your current account is, of course, your bank. It will do it if you go overdrawn – take out more money than you actually have in there – or break some other rule that you did not know about. Overdrafts used to be very expensive. They were how the banks paid for current accounts – the less well-off or badly organised paid for the better-off who were careful. Now banks can only charge you interest on the amount you are overdrawn for the time you are overdrawn. OK, it is typically around 39.9% interest, but overdrafts are – or should be – fairly short-term and the cost in pounds at the end of the month should not be that great.

You slip into the red on September 21 when your rent of £675 has to be paid but there is only £425 in your bank. The bank has agreed with you an overdraft of up to £1000, so it makes the payment. You now owe the bank £675 – £425 = £250. Then you take out £50 cash for a night out on Friday, but it gets a bit hectic and you pay for a couple of rounds with your debit card – another £37.14. You are now £250 + £50 + £37.14 = £337.14 overdrawn. Saturday you go out again and swear you will only take out £40 and stick to that. Which you do. So you are £337.14 + £40 = £377.14 overdrawn. On Sunday, you stay in and do not shop online. On Monday, your monthly pay of £1472 arrives and you are now in credit again with £1094.86 in your bank. That brief overdraft has cost you £4.55 in interest for the days you had it. Which you think is not bad. A couple of years ago it could have cost you £20 or more.

But 39.9% a year is a high rate of interest. It is fine for short-term debt for a few days. But do not make it a habit. If there's no money in your account, DON'T GO OUT! If you had an average of £500 overdrawn all year at 39.9% that would cost you £500 x 39.9% = £199.50 – just to pay the interest. You would still owe £500. So overdrafts are not good for long-term debt. Avoid them.

Earning interest on your account

Some current accounts do pay interest on your balance. It is always very little and always has limits on it – only the first £100 or only the balance between £1000 and £2000.

As I write, one well-known brand pays 5%, but only on balances up to £1500 and the 5% will fall to 0.25% after 12 months AND you must pay £1000 or more into the account each month. The top five such accounts all have complicated conditions. And they all change frequently.

I do know people – well, one person – who has multiple current accounts and moves money from one to the other to meet all the conditions and says he made £242 per month interest in 2017. But by last year that had fallen to just £46. He also made a few hundred pounds by switching from one account to another to get the switching bonuses. But unless – like Pete – you love nothing better in the evening than curling up with a warm spreadsheet, these accounts are a bit of a pain and you won't earn much on them.

Paying for your account

Overdrafts are less lucrative for the banks now. So they try to charge you for other things. Banks would, of course, love to charge us for our current accounts. But they face a major problem. Since Cooperative Bank used 'no current account charges' as a marketing tool in 1974, all banks have come to offer them for free. We now expect that in the UK. If one bank started charging, all its customers would soon migrate to a rival. So why don't they all decide to start charging on the same day? They would if they could but that is illegal. It is price fixing, market rigging and against competition law. So, they cannot collude to do it together and they dare not do it individually.

Instead, they are trying to insert it slowly into the market hoping we won't notice. And they have started with those readers who are at this moment shouting at this book 'What do you mean free? I pay for my current account.' I'm sorry to hear that because paid-for current accounts are generally very bad value. Let me tell you a story. A colleague of mine, a financial journalist, told me when I was ranting on about paid-for current accounts being a waste of money that he paid for his and he got useful benefits from it.

> *'For example,' he said, 'I get free breakdown cover. That is worth £80 a year easy. I also get travel insurance included.'*
>
> *'But Ben,' I said, 'you told me last week you don't have a car. And you also said you were saving up for a deposit for a flat and would not be going abroad this year. So you are paying £15 a month – £180 a year (banks always prefer to quote the monthly price because it sounds a lot less) – for two things you won't use. What else do you get?'*
>
> *'A £1000 no-quibble overdraft.'*

'So you can pay the bank more money!'

He cancelled it and moved to a free account the next day.

All the work that has been done on paid-for current accounts shows that in general the benefits are not worth having. For example, they often include mobile phone insurance when your phone is probably covered on your home contents policy – if you have one. And beware what any mobile phone insurance actually covers. Is it new for old or a refurb? How bad does the damage have to be? What if you left it in your car and forgot to lock it? Or you were drunk and it fell out of your pocket – you think? Travel insurance is always best taken out when you know you are going to go away, but if you are head of a family and you go skiing every year and hit the beach every summer, then it can be good value. But make sure it covers that bungee jumping and the snowboarding excursion up the slopes of Everest. As for breakdown cover – wait until you get a car and buy it separately. You may even find it comes as a perk with the vehicle for a year.

Paid-for current accounts have been widely mis-sold for years. If you have one that you did not want and were not warned about the costs of what it did – and didn't – include, then you may be able to get redress from the bank. There is a very good guide here:

moneysavingexpert.com/reclaim/reclaim-packaged-bank-accounts

Budgeting with banking apps

All banks now offer you some sort of online access from your mobile. But the best ones are the mobile-only banks, which offer everything that traditional banks do, plus they analyse your spending. There is nothing magical about this and some of the older banks do it too – just a bit more creakily. Every time you spend on your debit card, the bank is sent a long code from the merchant i.e. the shop, hotel, garage, pub, etc where you bought something. The first four digits of that long code (the Merchant Category Code or MCC) reveal the sector the firm is in. So the bank just has to use those to compile a pie chart of where you spent your money. For example, 22.7% in pubs, 13.9% on mobile phone charges, 15% in supermarkets and so on. **It is the best budgeting tool there is and if you need to save money, this really shows you the non-essential spending and how to reduce it.**

Some people don't like relying solely on one new digital bank. So they may still get their salary paid into their high-street bank and their essentials paid out from that account. Then all their spare money is transferred automatically to the new bank each month – in that case, the analysis of spending is just of their non-essentials. Still useful.

I confess here I still have an account with a traditional bank, but now use two app-only current accounts for special things. One of them is paying abroad. Most debit cards and credit cards charge you 2.99% just to use your card in a foreign currency, so when you are on holiday in another country or when you buy something in euros online. **New app-only banks, like Monzo, Starling and Chase, generally do not charge you that extra fee when spending abroad with a debit card – but check the terms carefully because they can change.**

Remember

- Current accounts are the workhorse of your finances.
- Direct debits and standing orders you can control.
- Continuous payment authorities must be stopped if you tell your bank to do so.

- Overdrafts are cheaper than they used to be but avoid them if you can – they won't help your credit score.
- It is almost never worth paying for a current account – most of them are free.
- Apps can be useful to manage your current account.

Boring bits

Before we go on, here's a word about cards:

- Debit cards take money out of your current account. It is your money. So when you buy something, you pay for it now.
- Credit cards are borrowing. When you spend money, you owe that to the credit card provider. You are spending money you do not own and will have to pay back in the future.
- Pre-paid cards are different. You load money onto them. When you spend, you are using money from the past.

PRE-PAID CARDS

Getting a current account can be difficult for some people. And they can be tempted into using an account that seems to be a current account, may even be called a current account, but is anything but. These are pre-paid cards masquerading as a bank account. You put money on the card and then you spend it using a card. However, these firms are not banks, even though they may offer you what they call 'banking' and say these cards provide a 'current account'. That is very dodgy marketing.

But hang on, you think, I pay money in and use a card to take it out, why is that not a bank? And even if it isn't, what's wrong with it?

Banks are heavily regulated and have to hold a lot of money in reserve so they cannot go bust. If they did, then your money is protected by the Financial Services Compensation Scheme up to £85,000 – way more than most current accounts hold! But these pre-paid cards are issued by firms that are regulated for what is called e-money transfer. They may not offer faster payments – paying someone or a firm instantly through your app – and they charge you for all sorts of things. Pay money in, take cash out, spend money, lose your card, use it abroad, do not use the account for many months – all these things may cost you money. So my advice is avoid them. They are expensive and insecure.

If it is hard to get a bank account because of your credit record or some bad financial management in your past, then go for a basic bank account with a bank. Almost everyone can get one of those. If you are refused, then complain to the Financial Ombudsman Service (see page 173 for How to Complain).

CREDIT CARDS

Credit cards are the banks' engines of profit. Used properly, they are brilliant. But you need to step surely and expertly around their canyons of debt. One major debt advice charity said that in 2021 two out of three people who came for help had a credit card debt and the average amount was £6,853.

Standard cards

You apply, get approved, you get a credit limit. Say £1000. You use the card to buy stuff but you do not pay then, it is a loan. You cannot rack up more than your credit limit in debt. In this case £1000. Once a month you get a bill for what you have spent so far and not paid off. You can pay off some of it or all of it. If you pay all of it on time, no interest is charged. If you pay less than all of it, then interest – average 26.6% – is applied to the whole lot. 26.6% is the annual rate, so you will pay 2% on your debt that month, which is added to what you owe.

0% purchase cards

These cards let you buy things but charge you 0% interest. That's right, no interest at all. But only for a limited period. Maybe as much as 24 months. Maybe just 6. It depends on your credit score. At the end of that time, you will start paying hefty interest charges on the debt you've built up. So only use them to buy something expensive and pay it off before that 24 (or 6) months runs out.

0% balance transfer cards

You can transfer the balance from an existing credit card and you will be charged 0% interest on the debt. However, you will be charged an upfront fee of say 3%. So if you transfer £1000 debt, you will actually owe £1030. The 0% offer will run out maybe after 30 months. That gives you time to pay the debt off. Use it for that. If you don't, hefty interest payments will start. The best idea is to cut the card up at the start and never use it. Just pay down your debt each month. Some cards do both 0% purchase and 0% balance transfer. I would avoid those as they just confuse things.

Credit builder cards

If you find it hard to get a loan or a credit card, these cards can help you get a good credit score. But always pay them off in full each month. Never pay interest, which is always at a super-high rate. Never be late with a payment or miss one. That will damage your credit score.

The good things about credit cards

- A credit card gives you interest-free credit up to a certain limit for up to 56 days. So, if you use the card and pay it off in full every month on the due date, you can borrow money for a short period at no cost. So they are best for people with enough money to guarantee that payment every single month.
- If you buy something for over £100 (but no more than £30,000), you get extra consumer protection so, if something goes wrong with what you buy, the credit card provider is equally liable with the retailer and has to refund you (more on this in Chapter 6 page 167).

Errr, that's it. Those are the good things about credit cards.

The OK-if-you're-careful things

- You can use a credit card to give you a credit record or improve a poor one, if you use it carefully. That means paying any debt off over a short period and ideally every month, and never ever being late or – aarrgghhh – missing a payment. That will give you lots of big ticks on your credit report and improve your score.
- Some credit cards – very few now – give customers a small bit of cashback or points (and what do points mean? Disappointment) on everything they buy. But unless you pay it off in full every month without fail, the points or cashback will be worth less than the penalty for late payment or the interest you are charged.
- Zero-per cent purchase cards let you shop interest-free for a longer period of time. But these cards are only useful for specific purchases when you want to spread the cost. Or if you know some money is coming your way but not just yet that you can use to pay it off in full

and in time. Remember at the end of the interest-free period, you will have to pay the whole lot off or start paying probably 26% interest on the debt.

- If you need to spread a debt out for a few months – say a new washing machine or a holiday – then credit cards are OK, but again only if you are disciplined and do pay off that debt quickly so the interest charged costs relatively little.

The bad things

- Credit cards advertise one rate – usually a good one – but all that means is that at least half those who apply and are accepted get that rate. You may be refused. Even if you are accepted, you have a fifty-fifty chance of getting a more expensive deal. Always treat advertised rates with great scepticism.
- When you sign up you can choose to pay it off in full every month (good if you can afford it) or just pay the minimum. The minimum is a bad thing. Very few cards give you any other choice – like paying off a fixed amount each month.

The ugly things

- Interest charges are very high. As I write, the data company MoneyFacts says it is 26.6%. In other words, if you borrow £1000 over a year, you will pay £266 in interest and still owe £1000. Some charge nearly 40%. A few charge even more.
- Miss a payment date even by a day – Zap! £12.
- Miss paying in full even by a penny – Zap! Interest on the whole amount you should have paid.

- Go over your credit limit – Zap! £12. Every time.
- Take out cash and ZAP! £3 every time. And more if you take out over £100.
- Use your card abroad – Zap! 3% of what you spend every time you use it.
- Watch out with minimum repayments. If you just pay the minimum, then your debt can go on for years and be very, very expensive. You can end up paying more in interest than you borrowed in the first place.

The credit card solution

There are two ways to avoid all these ugly things:

- Never take out a credit card. They are fine for better-off people who can pay them off each month without even noticing. Some even reward big spenders with discounts or cash back. But they prey on those who have very little by tempting them into debt and then charging them a lot for it.
- A pair of scissors. If you have a credit card, cut it into pieces. Throw the bits into the plastic recycling. Write down what you owe and work out how many months it will take you to pay it off. Set up a standing order and pay that much every month until it is gone. Sorted.

Oh no, not percentages!

Banks make their money because they are better at sums than the rest of us. I said on page 24 in Chapter 2 that budgeting was just adding and subtracting and we can all do that right? But then when you start borrowing or saving you will see – OMG – percentages. But really they are easy.

A rate of 25% means that if you borrow £100, it will cost you an additional £25 over a year. So instead of 25%, just say £25 per hundred pounds.

Nowadays, loans and savings must use a standard way of working it out in adverts. So when you borrow you will see the letters APR – annual percentage rate – after the percentage e.g. 17.9% APR. **You don't need to understand anything except this – the bigger the APR, the more expensive the loan.** A personal loan of 4.9% APR is cheaper than a credit card that charges 19.9% APR. Of course, those high-cost loans that are advertised on the TV, which can be over 1000% APR are very very very very very very expensive and you should always say 'no'. In fact, anything above 39.9% you should always turn down. That rules out pawnbrokers, buddy loans, payday loans and even some credit cards.

One well-known high-cost lender will let you borrow £500 over 13 weeks. Every week you pay £55 and by the end that is £715. So you have paid them £215 to borrow £500. The APR on that is 1557.7%, about the maximum the rules allow. Just say no. In fact, never even contemplate it.

BUY NOW, PAY LATER (BNPL)

Nowadays, every time you shop you will be offered a buy now, pay later deal. These are fairly new forms of credit and they can be good. But beware. They immediately pass the APR test – the interest charged is zero. Yes. Nothing. Zilch. You buy a nice suit for, say, £500. With Klarna's 'Pay in Three' option, you pay a third of the cost when you buy, another third 30 days later and the final third 30 days after that. The money is taken automatically on the due dates from the credit or debit card you use at the point of sale. So, for example, if you used it for your Christmas shopping in December you could spread the cost interest-free into January and February. The rate of interest charged is 0% APR. There are no fees. There is only one sanction. If you do fail to meet a payment, you are banned from using Klarna. For life. That alone keeps people paying. The danger is that people will overstretch themselves, get into difficulties and then borrow on a credit card or, worse, a payday loan, to pay off these 'interest-free' BNPL loans! That is madness. Others pay off the BNPL debt by not paying important bills like electricity or rent. And yes, they are more important than buying a new outfit. Honestly.

Other BNPL deals include Clearpay, which lets you pay in four instalments every two weeks and Laybuy, which divides the amount by six and takes them weekly. Neither charges interest but if a payment is late, then both charge a fee of £6, which can go up to £36 in total. That could be very expensive borrowing.

However, there is no denying that buy now, pay later can be useful for online shopping. Buy the same outfit in three sizes and four colourways and keep the one (or two) you like, sending the others back, often free, within the time limit (see page 171 in Chapter 6). The rest you never even pay for.

If you consider using buy now, pay later, there is only one question to ask yourself. Why? If you can afford it now, pay for it now. If you can't afford it now are you absolutely sure you will be able to when you have to pay?

A late payment might affect your credit score and ultimately all three send in debt collectors if you do not pay as you agreed and, at that point, costs could be incurred.

BNPL firms make their money by charging the shop a fee every time you use them. People tend to buy more than they would if they had to pay right away, so the shop is happy to pay the fee. They sell more stuff. The banks are also joining in this lucrative business. So your own bank or credit card may offer it to you as well.

Like any form of credit, BNPL can be good or bad depending on how you use it. The danger is that people use it to buy things they cannot afford now in the hope that in a few weeks they will be better off financially and will be able to meet the instalments. Sometimes they cannot.

If you use buy now, pay later you lose a valuable right called 'section 75'. If you pay by credit card for goods that fail to arrive or are faulty and the retailer refuses to refund your money, then the credit card firm is jointly liable and you can go to the provider to get your money back. Purchases using BNPL do not have these rights, even if you use a credit card to pay. BNPL firms may offer some protection but it is not a legal right. At the moment, BNPL is not regulated so if you have a complaint you cannot go to the Financial Ombudsman Service. By the time you read this, they may be regulated. But details are still awaited.

If you are a careful credit card user you can do just the same – credit cards were the original buy now, pay later scheme! – and you do get those valuable section 75 rights to a refund for faulty goods.

CASH OVER CARD?

I love cash. It is great. But I hardly ever use it now. And we are all using less and less of it. Of course, Covid meant for a couple of years we visited shops less and bought more stuff online and those habits have persisted. The amount of money taken out of cash machines is less than half what it was a couple of years ago.

But cash is still useful. If you are on a limited budget and you take your weekly money out in cash at the start of the week, then you can allocate so much for rent, so much for food, so much for bills, and the rest – if there is any – for fun. Cash is the physical representation of your wealth and it is a really handy way to manage it. Take out your debit or credit card. Look at it. It gives you no clue whether it is good for £25,000 or nothing.

Banks don't like cash. Well, it is expensive for them – they have to count it, handle it, move it, guard it, insure it and store it. All that takes time and time means money. And most of that work they do for free or very little. When you take £50 out of a cash machine or over the counter at the last remaining bank branch in the country, they do not charge you. So the banks came up with the best money-making wheeze – contactless payment. Now you can just hover your card over the card machine in a shop or pub and up to £100 can be spent without a PIN. It has revolutionised our attitude to cash even more than Covid. And why do the banks love it so much? Every time we spend even a modest amount – a magazine, a coffee, a bus fare – they get a tiny, tiny bit of what you spend. You don't pay that – the retailer does. The key to wealth is to take a tenth of a penny off everything everyone on Earth spends every day. You would be a billionaire in a day or two. And that is what the banks do. They snip off a teensy bit of our money every time we buy something. And it is easy for us too. But beware – it can lead you to spend more than you should because those smart cards are not yet smart enough to show your balance. So beware the freedom of cashless. Waving around a contactless card can mean waving goodbye to your money a bit too easily.

And talking of cash, some cash machines charge you. After many battles, they must show you the cost on the front of the machine in big letters before you even start to get your cash out. And it is a flat fee – maybe £1.85. So whether you are taking out £100 or £10 you will pay the same and have left £98.15 or £8.15. That last charge is a whopping 18.5% – nearly a fifth of the money gone to the machine provider. You can find your nearest free cash machines using the LINK app. Put in your postcode and find the nearest free (green) and paid-for (purple) cash machines, as well as post offices, which let you draw cash from your bank free over the counter. Some shops will now offer cashback to people who don't even buy anything. All on the LINK app. Don't pay for your own money!

NOTE These are the costs for using a debit card to take money out of your bank account. If you use a credit card (never ever do that!) you also pay £3 or more just to take out cash – see credit cards on page 63.

CREDIT HISTORY

Every time you borrow money, open a bank account, take on a monthly mobile contract, rent somewhere, sign up for electricity and many other normal adult financial deals, computers in three credit reference agencies churn into action. These agencies are Experian, Equifax and TransUnion. All are American but regulated in the UK. They store as much information as they can about almost everyone in the UK. The information can be used to work out roughly what your income is. They also know what credit cards you have, how much you use them and what the limits are. Late and missed payments are recorded. So are all loans, your current account and overdraft, a mortgage and so on. In many ways, this is a good thing. It means that when you go to borrow more or get another mobile or hire a car, the merchant can give you an instant decision. Are you a good credit risk? Should I lend them any money? Should I trust them to pay this bill? And the answer will come back at once – yes, no or maybe.

All firms want to get new business. But they do not want it to turn into bad business – someone who always pays late, someone who is not what or who they seem, and someone who will go bankrupt and not pay them at all. So they use data from your past to predict your future. And, of course, the past is not always a good guide to the future. You might be a perfectly good payer and reasonably well off, but then suddenly you fall ill, lose your job, get divorced or have an accident and bam! You want to repay your loan, find your mortgage payments, pay your energy bills but you just can't.

These facts are called your credit record. But it doesn't stop there.

Calculating credit scores

Credit reference agencies do the best they can to assess you from your past behaviour. If you have very little past behaviour on their records then that is bad news. They may just reject you anyway. So when you are young it is important to build up a good credit score. You can be turned down for credit – a card, a mobile phone, a rented flat – just because you have what they call a thin file.

The three agencies all work out what they call our 'credit score' – a single number that represents our creditworthiness. Each has its own scoring system and each has a different number for the highest score. But in general, they use the same data and similar methods. I describe the one used by Experian – at least as much of it as it has made public.

That score is affected by how we use our credit cards. First, it is good to have a high credit limit. Over £5000 you gain 20 points because your lender sees you as a good credit risk. But if it is £250 or less you lose 40 points. If you use more than half of that credit limit, your points start to go negative. If you use 90 per cent, you will lose 50 points but using less than 30% will gain you 90 points on the sliding scale – out of a possible 999 on the Experian scale.

The three agencies use different scales:

- **Experian** runs from 0 to 999 and you need 961 points or more to be excellent, and anything below 561 is very poor.
- **TransUnion** (which is also used by Credit Karma to give you a score) uses a scale of 0 to 710 and makes anyone below 520 very poor and above 627 excellent.
- **Equifax** now does a score out of 1000. Anything over 811 is excellent, poor is 438 or below.

So, you can easily be seen as a different credit risk by one agency or another. To top it all, lenders won't necessarily use these scores. Either they will have their own system of analysing the data or they will add different things. If they make their money out of people defaulting, then they will not want perfect payers.

How to get a good credit score

Get on the electoral register. I don't care if you hate politicians and think they are all the same and will never vote. Get on the register. Contact your local council. In fact, nowadays it will contact you. But if you move around a lot, you may still not be on one. It is the first thing they check. And it is worth plus 130 points.

If you have debt or a monthly mobile bill, or you pay for a TV service or electricity, never be late with a payment, even by a day or two. That means you lose 130 points off your score. And NEVER default, that means 350 off your score. Every time you are late or default, those computers will put an amber or red mark by your name, making it harder to get credit, including a mortgage when you want to (more about prepping to get a mortgage on page 142 in Chapter 6).

Run your bank account well. Money going in, money going out, preferably not overdrawn.

Take on a bit of debt. I know I have said avoid credit cards and debt if you can, but taking out what is called a starter credit card that you use a bit and always pay off every month without fail helps build up a good credit record.

But the golden rule is – have some credit, do not use all of it, and meet every payment in full and on time. Easy to say. But however hard it is to do, the closer you come, the better your credit score.

Accessing your credit data

Over the last few years, credit reference agencies have stopped working in the background of our lives, quietly giving banks and others private information about us so they can decide whether to accept us for a loan or product and if so, how much to charge. Now, they want to make more money out of our information that they hold. The first idea they had was to sell our own data back to us! By law you can get hold of your credit reference information for free. Just by asking. But you can also pay a monthly fee to have it nicely packaged with alerts by email every time it changes. Experian, for example, the largest of the agencies in the UK, will sell you your own data back for £14.99 a month or, as I would put it, £180 a year. It comes with alerts and advice on how to improve the score Experian gives you but £180? Really?

The second idea is to offer us free access to our credit score as worked out by the credit reference agency. It will tell you each month if it has changed and, if it hasn't, will probably tell you it might have changed so check it out. You can check it free, so what's the catch? It will use this monthly email as a marketing opportunity and say things like, 'Great news, people with an Excellent credit score like yours are typically seeing 37 credit cards they're eligible for when they search with us.' Other times they will offer us a great new 0% card (with a fee to transfer a balance) or a cheap loan offer. In other words, they turn your data into a big selling opportunity and, guess what, if you take up an offer they get a cut. Ker-ching!

As the old adage has it – if something online is free, then you're the product!

So, use these tools by all means but remember what they are for.

One final thing – student loans do not affect your credit score. However, the repayments are seen as an outgoing and leave you less income to repay a mortgage, so it may affect how much you can borrow. But do not worry that this is a big debt. Treat it like a graduate tax that ends after 30 or 40 years, depending when you started uni.

If you are a student with money worries, then the National Association of Student Money Advisers (NASMA) is a great place to start. They have people on every campus who can help with the practical and emotional strains of managing your money for the first time.

Remember

- You need a good credit record to take out a monthly mobile phone contract, a credit card, borrow money or even rent a place to live.
- There are steps you can take to improve your credit score – or build one up if you don't have much of one.
- You have a right to know the information credit agencies hold on you. You can get it free.
- Credit reference agencies will encourage you to take on more debt.
- Student loans do not affect your credit score.

WHAT IS INFLATION?

Ask your mum or dad about inflation and they may not know much about it. For most of their lives, it was not a concern. But at the start of 2022, it suddenly became an issue. Inflation is just the general rise in prices. For example, something you paid £10 for a year ago now costs £11. That is an increase of £1 out of £10 or a 10% rise. Which is about the current level of inflation. We have had high inflation before – ask your grandparents about the 1970s – but for most of this century it has been asleep. Now it has woken up with a vengeance.

It is easy to see how much the price of an ice cream or a mobile phone has risen. But how do we measure the overall rise in prices? That is a difficult job. So difficult that even the boffins at the Office for National Statistics struggle with it and produce three different measures. In September 2022, the rate of inflation was 12.6% or 10.1% or 8.8% depending on which measure you used:

- Consumer Prices Index or CPI (10.1%) is the most widely used. That is the one you will see each month on the news as *the* rate of inflation.
- Retail Prices Index or RPI (12.6%) is still used to work out, for example, the interest charged on student loans and the annual rise in the cost of train tickets.
- The one the ONS wonks prefer is called CPIH (8.8%), which is just the CPI but includes an allowance for the change in housing costs (hence the H) for people who own their own home. No-one really uses CPIH at the moment.

All these indexes use what is called a 'basket of goods' and every month the price of each of the 700 items in that basket is sampled. Add them up and that is how much prices have risen. So what items are in the basket? You may be surprised. Food of course. Petrol (even if you don't have a car the price affects everything that is transported by road). Mobile phones and broadband. Clothes. Furniture. Going out. Every February the items in the basket are changed slightly as tastes and what we spend our money on alters. In 2022, for example, frozen Yorkshire puddings, sports bras and kitchen bin liners were added (they know how to party at ONS!). But dictionaries, doughnuts and men's suits were removed. One of the items added – a climbing wall session – was much derided as the vast majority of us have never done such an activity. It just shows how difficult it is to make one index (or even three) reflect the actual rise in prices that any of us feels.

All the baskets used for the three indexes are similar – though the way housing is counted is the most different. The big difference between the RPI and the two CPIs is the arithmetic, which means that the CPI and CPIH are always lower than the RPI. Usually by about one percentage point, though nowadays it is more than that. The new arithmetic (see the box below for some extra nerdiness) is supposed to be more accurate and preferred by statisticians throughout the world. And the RPI has been demoted as no longer a 'National Statistic'. But it has been around for 75 years and is embedded in so many things ONS still calculates and publishes it every month. There has always been the suspicion that the government prefers the CPI method because it is always smaller. And when it uses it to increase benefits – which so far it has since 2011 – it costs it a lot less.

The new arithmetic

The difference between the RPI and the two CPIs is how prices are averaged. Normally when we say the 'average' we mean adding up all the different items and dividing by the number of them. So, the average of 3, 7 and 8 is 18/3 = 6. Technically that is called the 'arithmetic mean'.

But the CPIs use what is called the 'geometric mean'. To get that, you multiply the numbers together instead of adding them. Then you work out what is called the root. So 3 x 7 x 8 = 168 and then work out what number multiplied by itself three times (the number of items) = 168. That number is about 5.518. As you will see, 5.518 is smaller than 6. And that is why the CPIs are always smaller than the RPI.

NOTE Geometric mean is only suitable for amounts that are correlated. In other words, we expect prices to be rising or falling in a similar way. If there are wide differences, then the geometric mean is not good. But then the average can also be misleading.

INTERNSHIPS

Once you leave school or university, beware of internships – a placement in the business of your dreams, which you hope will get your career off to a flying start. However, young people are often exploited by firms, especially in the fashion or media industries. They can find themselves working for a month or even longer without pay. That is against the law. All workers should be paid the minimum wage and no reputable employer should profit from unpaid labour. **Someone aged between 18 and 20 who has been an intern for four weeks, working a 37½ hour week, should be leaving with just over £1000 after tax.** Many don't. One report in 2020 found that 43 per cent of students surveyed had worked for nothing, although it is against the law for companies not to pay workers.

If you do not have a written contract, but are employed to do work and expected to turn up and work for certain hours, then you have a verbal contract and must be paid. It is also wrong to dangle the prospect of a job as an inducement to work for nothing. Possible exceptions are:

- If you are not actually doing work, but just shadowing someone, it may be legal not to pay.
- If you volunteer to work for a charity, you may just be paid travel and food expenses.

Beware of unpaid internships that a relative or a friend of a friend finds for you. They could be illegal and also act as a barrier to social mobility, as unpaid internships are only possible where the young person can be kept by someone else, like parents or a partner.

If you are seeking an internship, check out the guidelines produced by the Chartered Institute of Personnel and Development at **cipd.co.uk** and search 'internships'. If you turn up with that guidance the firm will either send you straight home or respect you greatly! If you have been an intern and you were doing real work but were unpaid, you should go back and demand back pay for the time you were there. Do it in writing – by which I mean an email – and say if you are not paid you will report the firm to His Majesty's Revenue & Customs, which enforces the minimum wage laws. Go to gov.uk and search 'pay and rights'. Another very useful source for advice about problems with work or jobs is ACAS, which has a lot of information and advice at **acas.org.uk/advice**. Or you can call its helpline on 0300 123 1100.

INCOME TAX

Sorry, but we have to look at income tax. Ideally, the Treasury would like to take a share of every pound you earn. But politicians who claim not to want to tax us to death get in the way and the result is a huge and complex system of tax-free allowances and so on. And in a few paragraphs, I'll introduce you to the stealth tax called fiscal drag!

Each year you are allowed an amount of income before income tax starts. It's called your personal allowance and is currently £12,570. It may rise in the future. That is the amount of income you can have in the tax year before tax is due. What? What's a tax year? Ah. That is the 12 months between 6 April one year and 5 April the next. Why? Well, 270 years ago ... see paullewismoney.blogspot.com and search 'tax year'. It is more interesting than you might think!

Above that allowance, income tax is charged on every £1, so the Chancellor keeps 20p and you keep 80p. When your income exceeds £50,270, higher rate tax of 40% begins on everything earned over that amount. And a top rate (called additional rate officially for some bizarre reason) of 45%

is charged on income above £150,000 . Plans to scrap that rate were hastily abandoned in October 2022. On income over £100,000, you can end up paying 60p of every pound to the Chancellor because for every extra £2 you earn, the threshold falls by £1 and disappears completely if you earn £125,140 or more. That weird rule may also go in the future. In Scotland it is a bit different, starting at 19p in the pound on most income with you keeping 81p, but that soon changes to 20p and then 21p and higher rate tax of 41p in the pound begins at £43,662. Details in the boring bits box. If you live in Scotland, then in 2022/23 you will pay more income tax than in the rest of the UK if your income is above £27,850. Below that, you will pay less. These rates and bands in Scotland may change in 2023/24.

Boring bits

Income tax

- Personal allowance is currently £12,570 – income tax above that is 20%.
- The higher rate tax of 40% currently begins on income over £50,270.
- Personal allowance is reduced at the rate of £1 for every £2 above £100,000, a process that ends at £125,140 when you have no personal allowance left. This rule may change in the future.
- Between those two amounts, from every extra pound you earn the Chancellor keeps 60p and you keep 40p. No, it isn't fair but that is how it is.
- When your income tops £150,000, every extra pound is taxed at 45p.

Scottish income tax

If you live in Scotland, then the tax rates are different but only on some income, including earnings, self-employed profits, pensions and income from rents. All other income, such as savings interest and dividends, is taxed as it is in England. And yes, that does make the calculation very tricky! You will have an 'S' after your tax code:

- Personal allowance (the same) – £12,570.
- Starter rate 19% over £12,570 to £14,732.
- Scottish basic rate 20% £14,732 to £25,688.
- Intermediate rate 21% £25,688 to £43,662.
- Higher rate 41% £43,662 to £150,000.
- Top rate 46% over £150,000 (the same threshold).
- And the personal allowance is phased out just the same as in England from £100,000.
- All these bands and rates may change in April 2023.

Wales and Northern Ireland

Wales has some tax-changing powers but so far has chosen to use them to keep tax the same as in England. Northern Ireland does not yet have tax-changing powers, so income tax is the same as in England.

Losing a fifth of your money is bad enough. But as I explained on page 38 in Chapter 3, there is one more tax on your earnings.

National Insurance

National Insurance is another tax of 12% of everything you earn above £242 a week (or £12,570 a year). National Insurance is worked out weekly. The rate of National Insurance is 12%, though it was 13.25% from 6 April to 5 November 2022.

Income tax and National Insurance total nearly a third of your earnings above the personal allowance, currently £12,570 a year, which is snaffled by the government. There is a different rate of National Insurance for people who earn more than £50,270 a year (£967 a week). Oddly it is lower – just 2% of your wages above that level.

So, if you earn over £50,270 a year your total tax is 40% + 2% = 42% taken by the Chancellor.

So that is tax. It should be simple but generations of accountants and politicians have rendered it much more complicated. Other bits of income can also be tax-free and not count towards the allowances.

Tax and self-employment

Tax is a bit different if you are self-employed. When your side hustle turns into a business, then you must tell HMRC. You need to tell it by 5 October in the tax year after your business first turned over more than £1000. You will then be in self-assessment country and you probably need to talk to an accountant to keep things straight. My advice is to pay a third of everything that comes in into a separate savings account that you are only allowed to use to pay your tax when it falls due. Then you know that the tax bill will not become an expensive and frightening debt. In a way it is like PAYE – what you take home is less than your headline salary or wages. So it must be with self-employment.

When I was first self-employed, I rigorously put money into a special savings account called 'My Tax Bill'. It was a third of everything I earned in fees. That meant I had enough to pay my tax bills as and when they arose. I did that even if it meant I was a bit overdrawn. So, I broke my own rule (to be fair, I hadn't invented it then!). But having that tax bill money safe and secure let me sleep at night. A small temporary and occasional overdraft did not worry me. And cost very little then as it does now. I called that account my 'sleep at night money'. I don't enjoy paying tax, but it is a lot less horrid if you have the money to do it.

There is more on self-employment and tax in Chapter 5.

Marriage allowance

You are eligible if:

- you are married or in a civil partnership

AND

- your income is below the personal allowance, currently £12,570

AND

- your spouse does not pay higher rate tax

You can transfer up to £1260 of your unused personal allowance to them, so they pay £252 a year less tax. More on this on page 258 in Chapter 9 and at **gov.uk** – search 'marriage allowance'.

Savings interest

The first £1000 of savings interest (so you probably have more than £25,000 savings or rather more than that if it is not in a best-buy account) is tax-free if you only pay basic rate tax. If you pay higher rate tax, that £1000 is cut in half to £500. And if you pay top rate tax, then it vanishes to zero.

If your income is below the personal allowance (currently £12,570) then you can have another £5000 of interest above that amount and pay 0% tax on it. So, if your income is low but your savings are massive – up to about a third of a million – this is a useful concession.

Trading income allowance and property income allowance

If you have a bit of a side hustle and the income from it (not profit) is up to £1000, that is tax-free. If it goes over that, then you can just deduct £1000 from it and pay tax on the rest or do proper accounts and pay tax on your profits. Ditto property income, which basically means rent but you could get it by renting out your drive as a parking space or letting someone use your electric car charger for a fee.

Fiscal drag

Until this book was in its final stages, we thought all these allowances were frozen until 2025/26 and the earliest they would change was from April 2026. However, a period of political turmoil made that less certain. After resignations and a new Chancellor Jeremy Hunt in place it seems much less likely that these allowances will be increased in the near future, but they may be at some stage. If they are not, then, the dreaded stealth tax called fiscal drag is set to take a total of £46.8 billion off us before the allowances change again. By law, the main ones should go up each year with inflation. But to save money (£46.8 billion!!) the previous Chancellor Rishi Sunak (who then became Prime Minister) decided they would be frozen. So, in 2022/23 you paid £78 more tax than you should have and up to £396 more if you are a higher rate taxpayer. That in itself saved £2.8 billion. If the freeze does continue year after year, the total gained by the Treasury is estimated to be nearly £47 billion taken from us through the silent stealth tax of fiscal drag. At the time of (re-re-)writing, it is expected that allowances will be frozen in 2023/24 and probably in some subsequent years.

LOVE AND MONEY

No, not that! But how you arrange your affairs (stop it!) to make sure that your passion for each other is not undermined by dark suspicions that all is not fair in the finance jungle. Do not neglect your financial relationship or the other good things about it may be lost.

COMMON MISCONCEPTIONS

First up, there is no such thing as a common-law wife or husband – the idea some people have that if you live together long enough you are somehow 'married'. You are not. You are both single. There never really has been such a status in England and Wales (though lawyers will argue about that). In Scotland, there was such a status until 2006 called 'marriage by habit and repute' but even that has gone now, and so has the peculiarly Scottish marriage, which could be claimed if a woman was persuaded to have sex on the promise of a marriage that then never happened. Now, you are either married or you are not. And of course when I say 'married', I include civil partnerships of same or opposite-sex couples. The statuses are essentially identical. So forgive me all you civil partners if I use 'marriage' and 'spouse' to include you too.

Marriage gives you a lot of very special financial rights. Living with someone in a state of non-connubial bliss gives you nothing, zero, zilch. That is true whether you just share the decorating or make a dozen babies. You have no rights at all to each other's property. So when your unofficial arrangement comes to an end for whatever reason, you cannot claim support, half the TV, the second car (assuming you have a first) or a share of your partner's money, pension or house in the Algarve. Unless you bought them, of course, in which case they are yours, yours, yours. Harsh but that is how it is. Of course, if there is a baby or twelve then a deal has to be done for the parent who does not have care of them to pay the parent who does. But there is no maintenance for the parent at all.

It is different in Scotland. After a cohabitation ends, one partner can apply to the court for a lump sum payment that covers the financial loss of one partner or the financial advantage gained by the other as a result of the relationship. For example, if one partner stayed home and cared for the home and any children, giving up her prospects of a job, then that could be recompensed. And any property jointly acquired during the cohabitation should be split equally. There is also, of course, provision for child maintenance. But even the Scottish rules are a million miles from the clear rights that marriage gives.

DIVORCE

If you are married and it sadly (or indeed gleefully) comes to an end, then things are very different. England and Wales first. The moment you marry you get the right to half your partner's property if that marriage ends. It does not matter whether that property was bought together, inherited from your Aunt Felicity or was a business you ran before the happy day. With divorce (and I include the dissolution of civil partnerships in that word) that is the default position – add it all up and then half to one and half to the other. Of course, it may not be that simple and the way the law is interpreted may change as time passes, but that is the place to start.

Property includes – well, just about everything. Her collection of rare trainers, his collection of original Spice Girls memorabilia. The house either or both of them owns. The valuable Porsche that she will not let anyone else drive. That lock-up in St Albans where he keeps – well what exactly? And, to stop being trivial, your pensions, your savings and your investments.

Pensions deserve a paragraph of their own. They can be worth more than your home. If either of you works in the NHS, as a teacher or a police officer or anywhere in what is called 'the public sector', or if you work for a bank or insurance company or a big old firm that pays a pension related to your salary and years of service, that can be worth a good six-figure sum. There is an explanation of the value of these so-called defined benefit (or DB) schemes on page 219 in Chapter 8. And if one partner has this good pension and the other doesn't, then it should be shared. There are several ways of doing that and at this moment all I will say is get a lawyer and hammer it out. Sometimes it might be easier to *quid pro quo* it. You have the house, I'll keep my pension. But lawyers generally do not like those deals because the value of a pension is often underestimated. Make sure any bargains you strike are fair in the long-term. The important thing to remember as the confetti fades is what's yours is half mine. And that includes your pensions.

Divorce in England and Wales and Northern Ireland is now (since April 2022) much simpler than it used to be. There is no need to blame your partner or accuse them of being unfaithful or behaving unreasonably, nor do you have to wait for a long separation. It can all be done in as little as six months. But if you have property, assets or pensions, you do need advice and probably legal help to sort them out. Paying a lawyer an hourly fee for that advice is a sound investment.

In Scotland it is a bit different. Any property brought to the marriage or inherited from Aunt Kirsty stays with the spouse who brought it. The rights to maintenance for a spouse or children are also different in Scotland. It is even more important to get legal advice there, and the grounds for divorce have not been changed.

PRENUPS

Prenuptial agreements used to be ineffective in the UK. But now the courts can take them into account. And of course, in an amicable divorce so can the soon-to-be-ex partners. They are normally used if one person brings a lot more to the marriage than the other – perhaps a house or a second one, or personal wealth or indeed a business that they run. Be aware though that if you run a business and your partner looks after the children or the home, then the courts will say they deserve probably an equal share in the business as their work has contributed to your freedom to make a success of it.

These considerations are even more important in second or third marriages as the partners are likely to have more wealth and more commitments to their own children or other relatives. That will also have to be considered when the new will is drawn up. In England, Wales and Northern Ireland, a will made before a marriage or civil partnership is null and void once the nuptials have taken place. In Scotland that is not true, but it is still a good idea to revisit the wills. See page 186 in Chapter 7 for more details.

If you did not make a prenup but now wonder if it might have been a good idea, it is possible to make a 'postnup' agreement. But the courts are likely to be even more cautious about enforcing them, especially if they suspect that one spouse is exerting financial control over the other – see the section on coercive control on page 94.

SHARING AND CARING

How should we arrange our finances? That is very often asked when a couple first gets together. And no, I don't mean dating or that anniversary of – what exactly is it two years since? I mean physically getting together. Sorry, I'll start again – living together sharing a place, rented or bought, and all the common bills that involves. Broadband, rent, mortgage, water, council tax, electricity, gas, food, furniture, TV licence, Netflix or, if you're very well off, Sky. In other words, all those things you both use and both share and, yes, both pay for. Perhaps even a car if you actually share one.

Here is my solution. Keep your own money in your own account. If you both work, have your wages paid into your own account separately. Have your own credit cards. Then open a joint account for joint expenses. Work out the total of all that spending on utilities and food and other things that you both use. Divide the annual cost by twelve and then halve it. Pay that much each by standing order into a joint account. And then all those bills can come out of that account. You may need an extra bit at the start to make sure it doesn't go overdrawn.

Halve it??? Did he say halve it? But you earn twice what I do – that isn't fair. And what happens when I lose my job? Or those contracts stop coming in?

These are good points. How you divide the total is up to you. Is it by what you are paid? What you use – I never watch sport on Sky, you do all the time, besides, you eat at least 50 per cent more than I do, etc. Or more likely, just what feels fair to both of you. Or perhaps I should say least unfair to both of you. Because living with someone and sharing more than the odd night together can be a bit of a shock. But whatever you do, find an agreeable method and stick to it.

And then when you buy some unnecessary treat from what is left of your own money, only you can tell yourself that was a bit of luxury!

COERCIVE CONTROL

These rules apply equally to living together or marriage or civil partnership. If you cannot agree how to deal with money amicably or if your partner discourages you from working or having financial independence, then you may be experiencing what is called coercive control. Financial bullying is now legally part of domestic violence. It can be as damaging as physical violence. If you suspect it, then do get help and advice. The best is probably from the charity Surviving Economic Abuse **survivingeconomicabuse.org** and there are a lot of other guides to the signs of it happening. It often creeps up on people – and I have to say, like all domestic violence, it is usually done by men to women. So be aware of it if all is not amicable in the money conversations.

If you are looking for romance, then dating apps can be useful. But beware that many of the people out there and available are thieves. See page 130 in the Fraud section.

TAX ADVANTAGES

There are just a few tax advantages from getting married. If one of you earns too little to pay income tax, then you can give some of your personal tax-free allowance to your spouse or civil partner to cut their tax by up to £252 a year. Details on page 85 in Chapter 9.

If you pass property or money between you, there can never be any tax charged. This mainly affects the small minority of people who might be due capital gains tax. And when one of you dies – sorry, but it will happen someday – then if you leave everything to your spouse, no inheritance tax will be due and when they die, their heirs will get double allowances. At least that is how it is now. How it will be next century, who knows?

If you have never quite got round to marrying (or civil partnering) and one of you is dangerously ill, you can get an emergency or deathbed wedding. As the 90-year-old comedian Sir Ken Dodd lay dying in March 2018, an emergency vicar was called and a registrar abandoned the office and headed for his bedside. Ms Sybil Anne Jones, his partner of 40 years, became Lady Dodd and HMRC was denied an estimated £3 million inheritance tax as she inherited his assets tax-free, as his wife not his partner.

Deathbed weddings are not that rare and there are many reasons for them beyond tax planning. Like finally getting round to it or a declaration of eternal love while there is still time. They begin with a call to the local register office. All the normal restrictions of time and place for a marriage are set aside. The registrar will top up her emergency pen with indelible ink. And if the church is wanted too, the local vicar will don his or her emergency dog collar. It can all happen within hours if necessary.

STATE BENEFITS

If you live with someone, with or without a legal blessing, your entitlement to state benefits may change, especially if they are means-tested, like universal credit or pension credit. For benefits, marriage itself is neither here nor there. If you are together 'as husband and wife' as the law delicately puts it, then you are a couple and your income and assets will be counted together. For other benefits, it is less important but you should always check the financial implications of moving in with someone before stepping – or being carried – over that threshold.

Remember

- If you live with someone without being married or civilly partnered – same-sex or opposite-sex couples can do both now – you generally have no rights over each other's property or money, though the rules give you slightly more rights in Scotland.
- Living together means deciding who pays what and how that is fairly divided.
- Keep your own personal account for your spending.
- If it all goes horribly wrong, get advice about a fair and lawful division of your stuff.
- BUT if you claim benefits, the rules don't care if you are married or not – they will treat you as married if you are a couple.

CHAPTER 5

THE WORKING WORLD 23–41

Gosh. The last stage before middle age! This is the time to really get sorted. Make sure you are in charge of your money instead of the financial world being in charge of you. It is so key you get two chapters! This one about the bad stuff. And the next one about the fun.

Sorry to start here with some warnings about debt but it can be a killer. Later, I discuss money the government might give you when times get difficult and the money it will take from you when they are not. In fact, it may take it from you when they are difficult too! And then protecting your future.

I know at even 41 I wasn't sure how much I cared about reaching my sixties, which mainly seemed to happen to other people. But trust me, as someone who waved his sixties goodbye a long time ago, it does matter.

MANAGING DEBT

You are in the age of debt. To use the phrase of one of the firms that exploited people who needed to borrow – your month lasts longer than your money.

Now, there is nothing wrong with debt. Here is what you should do. Most people are paid monthly or weekly. But sometimes you just want or need something that cannot be paid for out of that money and you do not want to wait – take the waiting out of wanting as another tempting slogan once ran.

Let me tell you my golden rule of debt – if you borrow to pay for something, maybe Christmas or a holiday, never let the debt last longer than the next time you want that. So, your Christmas borrowing must be gone completely before next Christmas and that hot, lazy week on the beach must be all squared off before your next flight somewhere fancy.

If your bills are getting a bit difficult but not too bad, then the MoneyHelper website explains how to sort them into the most urgent and deal with those first. You can find it here:

moneyhelper.org.uk/en/money-troubles/way-forward/bill-prioritiser

With the cost of living rising, many more people are going to get into debt. It's inevitable. And sometimes debt becomes unmanageable. **Another golden rule is: if debt keeps you awake at night or if it is the first thing you think of when**

you wake up, then get help. And do it soon because if you ignore debt, like toothache, it only ever gets worse. If you tackle it head-on, then it can get better.

There are three places to go: all free, all charities, and none of them will judge you – they have seen much worse than your debt!

- **nationaldebtline.org** online or you can call free on 0808 808 4000
- **stepchange.org** online or call free on 0800 138 1111
- **citizensadvice.org.uk**, which has local centres in towns all over the UK and can offer face-to-face or telephone help

Never, ever google debt advice or debt help. You will get commercial companies whose aim is to make money from you. Use the charities listed above. They have lots of online help and advice and will find a solution to your debt. You may be able to do a deal with the firms you owe money to that will write off some or all of the debt. That should help you sleep well.

MoneyHelper lists other places to go but they are commercial companies and I would not recommend them.

DO NOT TOUCH – Gambling

I have never gambled. Except once. And I lost. So never again. It was an excellent lesson in my teens. Gambling is a very stupid idea. The bookies or betting sites always win in the long run. Even if you think you're very clever at poker or horses or spinning dials, the odds are rigged so that in the long run – and usually in the short run too – you lose. And if you are very clever and find ways round these rigs and start winning consistently, you will be banned. Because the last thing a gambling billionaire wants is a smarty-pants who beats them. So they ban you. Fair? Of course it isn't fair – it's gambling! The gambling industry in the UK makes £14 billion profit a year. That is £14,000,000,000 or around £300 for every adult in the country. It is a loser's game.

If you must gamble, and some people enjoy it, then decide you will bet an amount you can afford to lose – say £20 – and when it's gone, stop. Promise me you will stop. Don't chase your losses by thinking 'Just one more; I might win next time.' You won't. And that is the slippery slope that slides down to the worst thing about gambling – it can become an addiction that eats at your soul and takes all your money. Sometimes it leads people to take their own life.

Look at **stepchange.org** and search 'gambling'. Never google for gambling help because you won't find it. Citizens Advice is also good, as is **moneyhelper.org.uk**. There are several charities that can offer specific help. Most of them are paid for by the gambling industry, which rather puts me off, but GamCare (**gamcare.org.uk**) is probably the best or there is Gamblers Anonymous (**gamblersanonymous.org.uk**), which is a self-help organisation of people who have become addicted and overcome it.

My plea to you is to do something. It can ruin your life and those of people you love.

WORKING-AGE BENEFITS

I said in Chapter 2 that this book is not a complete guide to benefits. It can't be. But here we look at state benefits in (and out of) work.

Statutory sick pay

If you fall ill and you cannot work for more than four days, then your employer must pay you for the time you are off starting on the fourth day. It is called statutory sick pay (SSP) and is £99.35 a week. It lasts for 28 weeks. To get it you must be an employee, not self-employed, and earn at least £123 a week. It does not matter how many hours you work, you still get the same rate. If your employer sacks you while you are on SSP, it has to pay you as if you were not sacked. Many employers pay more than SSP, for example, they may pay full pay for a certain period, then SSP after that. You have to pay tax and National Insurance contributions on SSP.

Employment and support allowance

If you cannot work because you are ill long-term or have a disability, then you may be able to claim another benefit called new-style or contributory employment and support allowance (ESA). The same contribution conditions apply as for jobseeker's allowance (see below). You cannot get ESA as well as SSP, so to claim it you have probably lost your job or your SSP has run out. You can also claim it if you are self-employed. You may have to wait seven days before ESA begins. ESA is the same amount as JSA for 13 weeks while your capabilities are assessed. If the DWP decides you cannot prepare yourself for work, then you get an extra £40.60 a week called the 'support component'. If you do not get that, then you will have to do activities to prepare yourself to go back to work and ESA runs out in a year.

Otherwise, it can continue indefinitely while you get the support component. No extras are paid for children or rent or dependants, so if you need more money, you may have to go onto universal credit.

Jobseeker's allowance

If you lose your job then you may be able to claim jobseeker's allowance (JSA) – sometimes called new-style JSA or contributory JSA. This is paid if you have made enough National Insurance contributions in the two tax years before you lose your job, which is not a difficult test to pass. JSA is £77 a week (£61.05 if you are under 25) and is not means-tested, but it does come with tough conditions. As its name implies, you have to be seeking a job and prove it. You have to be available for work and submit to work-focused interviews at the job centre. JSA only lasts six months.

No extras are paid with JSA for children or dependants, but it is paid to you as an individual so if you live with a partner, that does not affect it. If you need extra money for children or to pay your rent, then you may have to claim universal credit instead.

UNIVERSAL CREDIT

If you are short of money – in work or out of it – then you may be able to claim a top-up from universal credit (UC). It is a means-tested benefit. In other words, the more income you have, the less you get. And if you have savings over £16,000 forget it – you cannot claim until they are below that. Even then your UC will be reduced until they fall to £6000, when they are ignored.

Another shock many young people find is that if they are in a couple, their income and savings are considered jointly. So if one loses their job, they may not get universal credit if the other is still in work and earning good money. This happens whether or not you are married or in a civil partnership. If you live together as a couple then your income and assets are counted jointly. This is one bit of finance where the status of marriage is irrelevant. I once had a friend who worked for what was then the Ministry of Pensions and National Insurance and his job was to assess the 'living arrangements' of people claiming what was then National Assistance. And yes, he could inspect what they called 'sleeping arrangements'. They are not allowed to do that now, but they are just as tough if you pretend to be single when really you are not. However, if you split up but remain in the same house or flat, you should be able to claim as a single person. But expect arguments and scepticism.

It is called 'universal' because it replaces six older benefits that you may have heard of:

- working tax credit
- child tax credit
- income support
- housing benefit
- income-based jobseeker's allowance
- income-related employment and support allowance

So if you pay rent and need help with that, then it is universal credit that you must claim. And if your contributory JSA or ESA runs out or isn't enough, claim UC to top it up.

Universal credit comes with tough conditions. And, no, it isn't called means-tested because the tests are mean! Though they can seem it. It also comes with some very odd jargon. So be prepared. It is a working-age benefit.

The moment you reach 66, you are a pensioner and claim pension credit instead, which is a lot better. But if you are in a couple, you cannot now get pension credit until you are both aged 66 or more.

Unlike other benefits, UC is paid monthly not weekly or two-weekly and it is paid in arrears. There is also an extra week you have to wait before even the counting begins. So when you first claim UC, you have to wait just over five weeks – a week plus a month – for your first payment. If you have no money at all, then you can get a loan to help cover the gap. But you then have to pay it back over the next year out of your benefit. In other words, you are borrowing from your future self, which means you are living on less than you need for all that time. So if you can manage without the loan – called a payment in advance – best to do without it.

So what can you get?

- If you are single, you will get £334.91 a month, but if you are under 25, the rate is only £265.31 a month.
- If you claim as a couple and either or you is over 25, then the rate is £525.72. If you're both under 25, it is £416.45.
- Savings (between you, if a couple) over £6000 will reduce the amount you get and savings over £16,000 means you cannot claim it.
- You get more for a child and for a second child but normally any other children are not counted unless they were born before 6 April 2017. The rules are complex and there are exceptions – often several – to every one of them. You can get more if you or a child are disabled.
- You can get up to 85 per cent of your childcare paid for children under 16 if you have a job or are self-employed.

If you do work, then you may get what is called a **work allowance**. That is the amount you can earn before your Universal Credit is reduced. Any money you earn above the work allowance leads to a deduction from your UC of 55 per cent of what you earn after tax and National Insurance contributions have been deducted. That means out of each extra £1 you earn, you only keep 31p – the Government snaffles 69p in taxes and reduced UC out of every £1 you earn. If you also get help with your council tax, then you keep just 24p. These calculations are explained in my blog – **paullewismoney.blogspot.com** – search '76% tax rate'.

Transferring to UC

People already on one of those older means-tested benefits listed above are being slowly moved to universal credit, which will eventually replace them. Transferring people onto it was paused for Covid, but from May 2022 the transfer of the remaining 2.6 million people began in earnest.

The Department for Work and Pensions says they will all be moved by the end of 2024. It also says that more than half of them will get more money on universal credit than on their old benefits. Just over a third will get less. **It is very important to check if you will get more or less – or the same in some cases. If you will get more then you could consider moving voluntarily. You do that just by claiming UC. If you will get less it is very important not to choose to move.** Wait for the DWP to make you change. Then you will be given extra money to make up your UC to what you get on the old benefits. This is called 'transitional protection' and will last until your circumstances change. That can include changing your address, having a child or no longer getting money for a child who has left home or is no longer a dependant. You will NOT get this transitional protection if you choose to move. So, wait until you are forced. You can check if you will be better or worse off with the benefits calculator at **www.entitledto.co.uk**.

Remember

- If you will be better off, consider moving to universal credit now but be aware it is paid monthly in arrears and comes with tough conditions.
- If you will be worse off, wait until the DWP says you must move and make sure you get the transitional protection.
- If you get transitional protection, try not to change your circumstances as it will disappear if you do and you will be worse off.
- This migration does not affect entitlement to contributory 'new-style' jobseeker's allowance and employment and support allowance.

Housing costs

Universal credit will pay a contribution towards your rent – in some cases all of it. But around half of all the people on universal credit do not get all their rent paid. They must find the difference out of their other money. If the place you rent has more rooms than the government says you need, you will have a deduction made for the extra rooms – dubbed the bedroom tax. If your rent is high and you have several children, then you can find that you hit what is called the 'benefit cap', which means you will get less than the normal figures show you should get. Neither the benefit cap nor the bedroom tax apply in Northern Ireland, where the Executive makes up the difference. If you have a mortgage, then you can get a loan to pay the mortgage interest or some of it.

You may also be able to get your council tax reduced on grounds of low income. Ask your local council about it. And remember, if you live alone, then your council tax should be reduced by 25 per cent anyway. In Northern Ireland, a similar scheme will reduce the rates you pay.

Conditionality

To get universal credit at all, you have to agree to certain conditions, the most stringent of which is to be available for work and actively seeking it. Basically, that means you must spend the equivalent of a working week looking for work or taking steps to make yourself ready for it. For the first month, work can be limited to jobs like the one you left. After that, it will mean any job. Unless you have children, you will be expected to find a job for 35 hours a week. That can be reduced to 16 hours for lone parents and some disabled people and if you have very young children or certain disabilities, you will not have to work or look for it at all. If you are self-employed, then after a year on universal credit you will be assumed to be earning the equivalent of minimum wage for 35 hours a week, which is £17,290 a year, even if the profit from your self-employment is less than that. To keep your benefit, you may then be forced to get a job as an employee. There is also something called in-work conditionality, which means even if you have a job, you may be asked to look for a better-paid one to try to get you off universal credit.

Co-operating

When you claim universal credit, you will have to report to a person called a 'work coach' and will have to start a diary online about your search for work. Unlike most diaries, it is not private. The coach can see it too and write in it and that is the chief way for you to communicate. You will need a smartphone so you can communicate with your coach and take instructions from them. You will also need a bank account for your money to be paid into. People who cannot cope with these demands may find it much harder to get the help they need and are entitled to. Ask for help at your local job centre.

More information

That was the briefest guide to working-age benefits. You can get help from **turn2us.org.uk**. It has a benefits calculator to see what you will get on various benefits. It also has guides to grants and other help you might get. You can also try the official website **gov.uk** – search 'universal credit'. Many people do not claim universal credit because of the hassle and the rules. But please don't be one of them. My taxes and yours are paying for it and I would hate them to be wasted. About five million people do get it and find it a lifeline in difficult times.

If you have a disability

I will be even briefer about disability benefits. The best guide to them is as long as this book and printed on A4. If you have any disability – physical, sensory or mental – the important thing to remember is that you probably can get extra help. Either a specific benefit like personal independence payment (PIP) if you need some help from someone else to live a full life. Or you may get additional amounts with means-tested benefits like universal credit. Always ask. And a good starting place is **turn2us.org.uk** or **citizensadvice.org.uk**, which covers the rules in England, Scotland, Wales and Northern Ireland very well.

TAXES

There is information about tax dotted about this book. Partly because what is important to you might change with your age. And partly because who would even open a chapter called TAX. Yuk! But it is important to understand it because basically it is the Chancellor slipping his hand into your purse and snaffling a big chunk of your hard-earned. So how does it work? I gave a lot of figures on page 82 in Chapter 4. But here is the process. If you are an employee, the Revenue likes to take the tax off your earnings before you see it through a process called PAYE: Pay As You Earn.

If you earn £30,000 a year, you will be paid £2500 a month. But you don't actually have £2500 paid into your bank account! Oh no. Before you see it, you will have £290.50 income tax and £174.16 National Insurance contributions deducted. If you pay into a pension, then you will also have that contribution deducted but you will pay a bit less tax. And if you are repaying a student loan, then there will be another deduction of at least £20.29 and up to £75.79, depending on which plan you are on. So, you will end up with a lot less than £2500 transferred to your bank.

More details on page 82 in Chapter 4.

Self-employment and tax

Self-employed people pay tax differently. **There is no PAYE** so it is up to them to work out what they owe at the end of the tax year. They then pay it through a process called self-assessment in the January after the end of the tax year the previous April. **Income tax thresholds and rates are**

the same (see the boring bits box on page 82) but National Insurance is slightly different. First, in 2022/23 it has to be paid on profits for the year over £11,908. From 2023/24, it will start at the same level as the income tax personal allowance, currently £12,570.

There are two sorts of National Insurance that must be paid when profits exceed the threshold:

- **Class 4**. This is 9% (rather than 12% for employees) on income between the tax threshold and £50,270. In 2022/23, the effective rate over the year was 9.73% as the rate went up and then down again during the year. Above £50,270 it is the same 2% National Insurance but over the tax year 2022/23 the rate used is 2.73%. These contributions do not entitle you to a state pension.
- **You also must pay a fixed-rate Class 2**. This is a contribution of £3.15 a week. That does count towards a state pension and if you have profits between £6,725 and the tax threshold, your entitlement to a state pension is protected for those years. If profits are below £6,725, Class 2 contributions can be paid voluntarily to keep up entitlement to the state pension. In earlier tax years, there were no credits and Class 2 was paid from around £6,500 a year. Class 2 contributions may change from April 2023.

Both Class 2 and Class 4 National Insurance contributions are paid by self-employed people on their self-assessment form after the end of the tax year.

Working from home

If you have worked from home since the start of the pandemic, you can claim a bit back from the taxman. Don't get too excited but it is worth doing. If your employer told you to work from home because of the pandemic for just one day in the tax year, you can claim the relief for the whole year. Mad? Yes. But it was a Covid concession. It applies in the tax years 2020/21 and 2021/22. The relief is £6 a week – in other words, you do not pay tax on £6 of your income. As it is for every week of the year, it means £312 of your income over the whole tax year is free of tax and you will pay £62.40 less tax in each of those two tax years. If you claim it now, you will get a cheque. If you pay higher rate tax, the relief is worth twice as much. The amounts are slightly different in Scotland and range from £59 to £128.

If working from home costs you more than that – and it probably does – then you can claim tax relief on what you actually spent. But – and it is a big but – you will need receipts.

If your employer pays you extra for working from home, you can still get the £6 tax relief. In normal non-Covid years, you only get the relief for each week you actually have to work from home. And the rules about what 'have to' means are strict. Go to **gov.uk** and search 'working from home'. There are other things explained there that you might be able to claim too – such as membership of a trade body or essential periodicals or books. All worth doing.

Tax code

Your employer has to deduct income tax, National Insurance contributions and student loan repayments. They do that using what is called a tax code. Each year you are allowed a certain amount of income before you pay tax. Currently it is £12,570 but may rise in the future. That is turned into a tax code by knocking off the last digit and adding a letter. Normally it would be 1257L. That means the first £12,579 of your income is free of tax. The '9' is used to bias it slightly in your favour. The code might be less if you have more than one job or a job where you get benefits such as a company car. It is also affected if you are married or civil partnered and one spouse has transferred part of their tax allowance to the other (see page 85 for who can do this). That will add an 'M' or an 'N' to your code. If there is an S, it means you are a Scottish taxpayer and a C (for Cymru) means you are a Welsh taxpayer. At the moment, Welsh income tax is the same as England's. If you want to know more, look at **gov.uk** and search 'tax codes'. Each year HMRC should send you a form called a P60 to tell you how much tax you've paid. When you leave a job, you get a form called P45, which shows what tax you have paid in that job.

THE WORD I CANNOT USE

This next section is about something that you will just have to guess. Do not use that word I was told! The p***** word. And no, it is not rude but the p***** word puts people off. But why? It must be important. The Government pours £38 billion a year into boosting whatever we save. That is nearly as much as the defence budget! So why do our eyes glaze over when we read the P word. **Pensions.**

A pension is a simple idea. But decades of hard work by the finance industry and numerous rules by the regulator not to mention tweaks by successive chancellors have turned this simple idea into something that makes even my eyes glaze over.

But it is simple. Trust me. Imagine a pot. I always think of the kind of pot Winnie-the-Pooh got his head stuck in. A Hunny Pot. But we'll call it a pension pot. Now write your name on it. That is your pension pot. At its simplest, you put money into that pot every month. The Chancellor puts some in too – a quarter of what you put in. So you put in a hundred pounds and suddenly there is £125 in there.

Magic, eh? I'll explain why it's £25 a bit later (see tax relief on page 118). Month after month, money goes in. There is a team of people in charge of that pot and they work very hard to make your money grow. They invest it. If you look carefully, apart from the big friendly rim round the top where you pop in four tenners and the Chancellor pops in another, there are half a dozen little taps at the bottom of the pot. And although it is your pot and your money, you do not control those taps. They are there to let some of your money out to pay the people who look after it. These taps should be labelled:

- annual management charge
- policy fees
- fund manager
- custody
- transaction costs
- trading fees
- bid offer spread
- ongoing charges

Your pot may not have all of these – and they are usually invisible and not labelled anyway – but it will have some. And like a honey pot left on a lawn, your pension pot provides food and a living for all sorts of creatures, each with their own tap. None of these charges reflects how well your fund grows. It can rise with the markets or fall with the crashes but all these parasites – and I use the word in the friendliest and biological sense – feed off your money. Over your lifetime, the growth in your money is enough to feed them all. But the meaner you are to them, the more you will have at the end.

You can't control how your fund grows. Or what the world economy does. Or changes the Chancellor might make. But you can control the charges by picking a pension with the lowest possible ones.

Taking control of your pension

Here's why it matters. Suppose your pension fund grows by 4% a year. And suppose the drips out of all those little taps amount to 1.5% of your fund every year. You and the Chancellor put in £125 a month from the age of 22 to the age of 65. At which point, you break your pot to see what you have to live on for the rest of your life. Your fund will be worth around £117,000, of which you have paid in £66,000. But the charges dripping out the bottom over the year will have cost you nearly £63,000 in the money taken (£32,000) and the lost growth. That is almost everything you have paid in. If there had been no charges, you would have had £180,000. More than a third of your fund has gone to 'them'. Suppose the charges were just 0.5% higher at 2%. That would have cost you another £11,000. More than 43% of your fund has gone to 'them' and 57% to you. If they were 1%, then only a quarter of your fund would have gone to them. **You cannot control the growth in your fund. You can control (a) how much you put in and (b) how much they take out. Every fraction of a per cent shaved off the charges is thousands of pounds in your pensioner pocket.**

Investments are one thing where you do not get what you pay for. There is not a shred of evidence that paying a lot to these people to manage your money makes it grow faster. You want the lowest cost fund you can find. Of course, the finance industry makes it hard to see what the total charges are. But work at it and find the cheapest. It is one thing you can control.

So that is the simplest pension. One that you just pay into yourself. Nowadays, often called a Self-Invested Personal Pension (SIPP).

Auto-enrolment

Nowadays everyone in work aged 22 or more pays into a pension run by their employer. The process is called auto-enrolment (AE) and it relies on our general inertia when it comes to money by automatically putting us into the scheme and hoping we won't notice. Most of us don't. Since auto-enrolment an extra 10 million people have started paying into a pension. You can opt out but if you change jobs or after three years, you will be opted back in and only then can you opt out again. Most people don't bother and that is a GOOD THING. **However, there are problems with auto-enrolment.**

First, the amounts going in are tiny. Officially they are called 8% of your pay but that is untrue. Officially that is split between the employer who pays 3% and the worker who pays 5%. These are untrue as well. In fact, the percentages are applied to our earnings above a lower limit, currently £120 a week/£6240 a year. So, if you are only earning, say, £240 a week/£12,480 a year, only 4% of that will be going into your pension. The very most that can go in – because there is an upper limit as well – is 7% of your pay if you earn £50,270 a year. For those working full-time on minimum wage, it is just over 5% of your total pay that goes in – split 3.6% from you and 2.8% from your employer.

Compare that with the 20% of total pay that should be put aside to ensure you have a pension of two-thirds your pay when you retire. Teachers, for example, pay in 7.4% of their pay and their employer pays in 11.7% – that is a total of just over 19% of pay. With auto-enrolment, you get a quarter of that and – guess what – your pension pot when you retire will be a quarter as big. Or less. The Bank of England, which probably has the best pension of all, puts in 51% of pay.

How much should you pay in? The simple rule is to pay in as much as you can afford from as young as you can. Simple but, like many things in finance, not easy.

Fiddly bits

There are two groups left out of auto-enrolment:

- Those earning under £10,000 a year do not have to be auto-enrolled by their employer at all, nor do those under 22 or over 66. They can choose to join and if they earn at least £6240 and are under 75, they will get the employer contribution.
- People earning under the personal allowance, currently £12,570 (£242 a week), earn too little to pay tax. They can miss out on the subsidy that the government gives to pension contributions (see tax relief on page 118). There is a simple way to solve this problem but the government has now decided on a complicated solution that will start from April 2024.

The second problem is that you have no say in which pension provider manages it for you. Your employer chooses. Pension providers are much of a muchness except in one thing – charges. But your employer gets to pick that not you. And you may find that the firm organising your pension is chipping away at its value each year by taking a big percentage of your money – *your* money – and you have no say in how much.

Third. When you leave a job, your pension does not move with you. Normally your pension stays with the scheme your old employer chose. It may not be possible or easy to move it to your new employer's AE scheme. This can mean you accumulate a lot of pension pots during your working life (see pension tracing on page 179).

Ask the boss

One way to boost your pension is to ask your employer if they will put more into it if you do. Some employers are very good about matching the funds going in. If it is a big firm, go to HR and ask about your pension options. If it is not, then ask your manager – or the boss themselves. Of course, the answer may well be hollow laughter. But it is worth a try. Alternatively, you can start your own pension side-by-side with your auto-enrolled pension – a SIPP, which I mentioned above.

When you reach pension age – or the age you want to stop work – then you can break open your pension pot and see what is in there. Then you have to find a way to use that money to eke it out and give yourself as good a life as you can. More on this on page 218 in Chapter 8.

The best pension scheme

So far I have talked about a pension pot scheme. They are not officially called that. The name is 'defined contribution' scheme, usually abbreviated to DC to make the adviser feel knowledgeable and you to feel confused, if not small. That is because the amount you put in is what you control or define. I know. It is silly. But the term was only invented recently to distinguish these pensions from the Rolls-Royce of pensions. Just like the word 'analogue' was invented to describe watches with a dial after digital ones were invented in 1972.

The other sort of pension – the best pension in my view – is called a DB scheme. That stands for 'defined benefit' because, unlike the pension pot scheme, you do not need to know what you put into your pension. Instead, your pension scheme tells you at the start what you will get out of it. So the benefits are defined not the contributions. They are also called final salary schemes.

At one time, this was just about the only sort of pension scheme there was. Most firms had no scheme at all but those that did had what was called 'superannuation' and if they did, employees had to join. One might be called an 80ths scheme, which means for every year in it, you get 1/80th of your pay when you retire. So, after forty years you would get 40/80ths, which is one half. You retire on one half of your pay and never need do another day's work. That is how pensions should be. In the past, that was half your pay at retirement. But nowadays, many have lessened the cost by making it half your average pay during your time in the scheme. These are still good schemes to belong to. And at least some of your pension will be given some protection against inflation.

Nowadays, you will find these pensions mainly in the public sector. Police, teachers, nurses and civil servants all have them. And we know they are the best pensions because Members of Parliament also have them. Outside the public sector, they are becoming rarer. Most are closed to new members. But some are not. If your firm has one of these schemes, join it at once. You will get far more out of it than you put in.

What is tax relief?

The government subsidises the cost of pensions in two ways. First, the funds that the pension money is invested in pay no tax on the dividends or other returns on the investments. We need not worry about that, it just happens. The big subsidy though – estimated at £38 billion a year – is that when you pay into a pension, the government gives you back the tax you have already paid on that money.

I earn £30,000 a year. I pay income tax of £3486 on that and National Insurance contributions of £2666, leaving me with £23,848. If I then pay £1000 of that money into my pension, the government puts in another £250. So my pension fund gets £1250. 'Hang on a minute,' you ask. 'Why £250? I thought the basic rate of tax was 20%?' It is at the moment. And if I have £1000 left after paying that tax, I had £1250 because £1250 x 20% = £250. So, the Treasury gives back to me the £250 in tax I have paid in order to have £1000 left. Don't worry if you don't follow, it gets more complicated. If I earn £60,000 a year and pay 40% tax, then to have £1000 left I have earned £1666.67 (check it: £1666.67 x 40% = £666.67). So if a higher rate taxpayer puts £1000 into their pension, the subsidy is nearly 67%. The top rate of tax is 45%, which means a subsidy of £818.18, nearly 82%, on top of every £1000 put in.

So, of course, higher and top rate taxpayers pile money into their pensions. That is why the government has imposed limits on that. You cannot put in more than you earn. And you cannot put in more than £32,000 in a year – which with the current Treasury top-up comes to £40,000. There is also a lifetime limit (called a lifetime allowance) of £1,073,100. That limit is on the actual value of the fund, not just what you have put in. And, of course, there are endless complex rules that allow some people to go above this amount. These allowances may be changed in the future.

But what about National Insurance contributions? Are they not part of this? Normally no. But then some wag dreamt up a wheeze so they could be. It is called salary sacrifice. You give up part of your pay, say £1000, and that goes into your pension attracting the usual tax relief. Because you are paid £1000 less, your National Insurance contributions bill falls too. And yes, the arithmetic is too complicated to do here. But if it is offered, consider it seriously. Remember though that you do have to give up that £1000 and when it comes to getting a mortgage, for example, your pay will be £1000 less than it was.

Scottish note

In Scotland the rates of income tax are different. Higher rate tax is 41% and top rate is 46%. So the subsidy to well-paid Scots is slightly higher at roughly 69% and 85% of their contributions from their taxed income. For people below those levels, it is paid at 20% and that is true whichever of the three rates of tax – 19%, 20% or 21% – you actually pay. But if you earn over £25,688 and pay tax at the Scottish intermediate rate of 21%, you can claim the extra 1% tax relief. Many people don't bother. These rates and bands may change in 2023/24.

Remember

- If you pay into a personal pension, keep costs as low as possible. It is the one thing you can control.
- If you pay into a pension scheme at work, your employer will add more money to what you put in.

- Always join a pension scheme at work – if you don't, you are turning down a pay rise.
- Everything you (and your employer) put in to a pension scheme has extra added by the government. It adds more if you pay higher rates of income tax.
- When you move jobs, see if you can move your pension to your new employer. If you can't, keep the paperwork to help you track it down when you reach pension age.

SAVING AND INVESTING

We're all told to do it. Save. But for many that is an impossible dream. In many cases, half the money they take home goes to the landlord. After tax and National Insurance, getting to work, buying tea and coffee, buying clothes and cleaning them, hair and personal care, oh, and food to eat and drink, with perhaps occasional socialising, there is not much left to save out of the share of your wages the landlord lets you keep.

One popular rule is called 50-30-20. You divide the money you earn into three pots. Out of every £100, half, or £50, is for your needs. £30 is for your wants – things you would like to have but, be honest, don't actually need. And the final £20 you use first to pay off any debt then, when that is done (a girl can dream!!), you save it.

At your age, you may not have the means to save much or invest long-term. Before you think of investing sort out your finances:

- **Pay off debt.** You will always pay more interest on your debts than you will earn on investments. So, if you have a credit card with a £1000 balance on it that will probably cost you at least £250 a year. If you invest

£1000, you will be lucky to earn much more than £25 a year. So 'investing' that £1000 by paying off your debt is the best use of any spare £1000 – or £100 or even £1 – you have.

- **Keep some money in cash.** Just when we think we're sorted, life chucks some muck over us. It could be illness, an accident, losing your job or even something nice like a baby on the way or indeed a wedding. So you need a bit of money – ideally three months pay – just to tide you over.
- **Pay into your pension.** It is the most efficient way to save. Your employer will pay in too and the Chancellor will boost the whole lot by 25%. Win-win.

Then read the stuff about investment on page 195.

ISA NONSENSE

ISAs – individual savings accounts – are very heavily promoted by the Government and by the financial industry. But for most people, most of the time, saving or investing in an ISA is a waste of time. If it is a cash savings ISA, you may end up worse off than if you had just picked an ordinary savings account.

Cash ISAs

An ISA is simply a cloak of invisibility, which hides your money from the taxman. They are only worth having if the amount of tax you will save is more than the premium price you pay for that magic garment. More than four million people put money behind the ISA cloak, even though they pay no tax because their income is too low! For them, they are literally pointless. Even the millions of others who do pay income tax may also be losing money by choosing an ISA.

Suppose you put the maximum £20,000 into a one-year fixed cash ISA. As I write, the best pays 3.9%, bringing you in £780 in the year hidden from HMRC. But if you find the best-buy one-year fixed rate savings account without the magic ISA acronym, you can get 4.5%. If you pay no tax, that will bring £900 over a year – £120 a year more than the ISA. If you pay basic rate tax, you will get £720 after tax from the regular savings account, which is almost as much as the cash ISA pays. In the past, basic rate taxpayers have done better in non-ISA accounts and may do in the future. Check current rates carefully.

And it gets worse. Even if you pay tax, you may still pay none on your savings interest. That is because there is a personal saving allowance, which makes the first £1000 of interest tax-free anyway for basic rate taxpayers. The figure drops to £500 tax-free for those who pay higher rate tax and to zero for the lucky few who have an income in excess of £150,000. A basic rate taxpayer would need around £22,000 in the non-ISA one-year bond to use the £1000 allowance – assuming they have no other savings – and a higher rate taxpayer would need around £11,000. The average value of a cash ISA is £12,400. Again, pointless.

Higher or top rate taxpayers who have used up their savings allowance and want instant access to their money should consider buying £50,000 of premium bonds, which can be cashed in at any time. Since October 2022, the interest rate is 2.2% tax-free, which is used to form the prize fund. Someone with the maximum £50,000 can expect to win every year on average three or four £100 prizes, the same number of £50 prizes and between 17 and 18 prizes of £25. The total average annual return is £990 in those tax-free prizes. For a higher rate taxpayer that is equivalent to 3.3% in an instant access taxable account and for top rate taxpayers it equals 3.6% taxable. Occasionally – every 15 or 45 years – you might win £500 or £1000, but don't count on it! It is not so good for a basic rate taxpayer of course – the tax-free prizes are the equivalent of just about 2.5% taxable return, which may or may not be competitive when you read this.

For information about Junior ISAs, see page 15 in Chapter 1 and more on Premium Bonds in the investing chapter on page 201.

Investment ISAs

Investment ISAs are also a waste of time for most people. Everyone gets a tax-free allowance on dividends of £2000. So for the ISA invisibility cloak to be worthwhile, dividends earned must exceed that. Suppose your investment tracks an index that pays dividends of 3.6% a year and total charges are 0.76%. Then to use up your £2000 tax-free allowance would require around £70,000 invested. Which is rather more than the average stocks and shares ISA in 2018/19 (the latest figures) of £64,473. Again, for most people the magic cloak comes at too high a price.

ISAs can be good value for top rate or higher rate taxpayers with very large amounts invested or saved. But for most of the rest of us mortals, they are a bit of a con. So always check to see if there are better deals before paying extra to wrap your money in the cloak of tax invisibility.

Innovative Investment ISA

I will just mention this as we pass by – the so-called Innovative Investment ISA. Do not be tempted. They are tax-free but by no means risk-free and the promised (not technically guaranteed but hinted at broadly) returns may not be achieved.

Lifetime ISA

One ISA that is worthwhile but only if used properly is the Lifetime ISA, also known of course as LISA – and don't ask me if it is pronounced 'Lisa' or 'Lisa' because no-one knows. LISA is tax-free on steroids. Any growth is free of tax, of course, and for every £100 put in the government adds £25.

The maximum investment is £4000 a year (out of your £20,000 annual ISA allowance) and so the maximum bonus from the government is £1000 a year. It is so good that there are tough restrictions: First your age – you must be aged 18 to 40 to open one and then can only put money into it up to the age of 50. Second, you can only use it for two things:

- Buying your first home (with a maximum price of £450,000).
- Putting towards your retirement, which means you cannot take it out until you reach 60 (or are terminally ill with less than a year to live).

If you break those rules, you are fined 25% of the total in the LISA, including the government bonus. Say you put in £1000, the total will be £1250 – if you take it out against the rules, you end up with £937.50. Remember that even if you can afford to salt money away now for that house deposit or the age of 60, life often intervenes – illness, unemployment, a wedding or just paying your fuel bill. A lot of people who put money into a LISA but then needed it for something else have paid that fine. But in the year 2021/22, 50,800 did take the money out to help buy their first home.

**IT'S A LIE.
AND THE PERSON
SAYING IT IS A THIEF.**

I interrupt this easy-flowing life to alert you to thieves. They are everywhere. Lurking in cyberspace, hidden behind masks that look like your bank, the police, your broadband provider, DVLA, HMRC, even your best friend. Anyone you might trust. But they all have one purpose. To rob you. Robbery without violence is a massive crime. And generally goes uncaught and unpunished. Just as people walking home at night used to carry swords or pistols to protect themselves against footpads or pickpockets, now we must never ever wander about online without being vigilant and taking a weapon of our own.

Nearly five million people a year lose money to what is politely called fraud or a scam. It is 42 per cent of all crime. Luckily there is one irresistible weapon that stops all fraud. And we carry it with us all the time. Your finger. If you get a call from someone you are not expecting and do not know personally, or a text from a firm or official, or an email from someone strange, then press end call or delete with that magic finger. Do not engage with it for one second. Delete it. If you are concerned it may be from HMRC – which confesses that there are 26 separate occasions on which it may text or call you without warning – or your bank or even your daughter or mother, treat it exactly the same. And then find a number yourself for that authority or firm or individual and call them yourself.

In the past, we used to say leave five minutes before making the call as phone lines did not disconnect immediately and you could find yourself talking to the thief again when you pick up the phone. Nowadays, that should not happen. But to be safe, leave it a few minutes – it helps gather your thoughts anyway – and if possible make the call on a separate line: another mobile or, if you still have one, a landline. Because one thing such a call tells you – the thieves have your number.

No-one ever lost money by cutting off a cold call or deleting a text or an email. Every week I hear from people who have not done that. And have lost in moments what it took them all their life to save.

Of course, the thieves try to find their way around this barrier. They can spoof the caller ID system so their call appears to be from your bank. Yes. That is right. The caller ID number may be fake. Never trust Caller ID. They can insert a text into a stream of text messages that you have had from your phone provider or electricity company so you think it is genuine. Or they can use stolen data to send you emails that appear at first glance to be from someone on your mailing list. Do not be fooled. Never respond. Never click on a link. And never listen to what they say. The moment you engage in conversation you are entering their world. And they know their way round that dark and friendless place better than you. By refusing to engage for a second you build an impenetrable barrier around yourself. A medieval castle that the outlaws and thieves cannot storm.

Sadly, these thieves are also cleverer and faster than the people whose job it is to try to catch or stop them. They will seldom be caught and never be stopped. Theft is a feature of instant personal communications and instant payments. We all want that convenience. And these low-lifes attach themselves to it like the parasites they are and try to suck out the lifeblood of our money.

The cleverest ones make us help them by persuading us that they are our friends against the thieves. This kind of theft goes by the unhelpful name of Authorised Push Payment fraud. Or APP. In 2021, nearly 190,000 people lost more than £500 million to it. Less than half was ever recovered.

- **Step 1** is an innocent call from someone you might trust – your bank, Microsoft, your broadband provider, the police – and as I said, the number showing on caller ID may be spoofed to be the same as one of those trusted parties. The thieves might ask you to check they are calling from the right number like a magician asks you to look under the cup when the ball is already in their pocket.
- **Step 2** is to warn you that there are thieves about (as indeed there are!) and that your money is at risk (as indeed it is!). They will ask you questions and tell you things that you think only your bank/Microsoft/BT would know. In fact, they are using a bit of leaked data and a lot of talent to get you to confirm things to them. When magicians do it this is called 'reading the subject'. They are building up your trust. But also frightening you.
- They use that fear to move to **Step 3**. You are afraid that your money is at risk and are convinced they can save it for you. They get you to embark on moving your money to a safe account that they have kindly set up for you. It may be in your name or appear to be. It may be an account you have moved money to before or appear to be. And you will pass on to them the code your bank sends to your phone. You are letting them steal your money.

- **Step 4** may well happen after the end of the call. Using the information they have obtained, they carry on stealing your money until it is all gone.
- **Step 5** is your epiphany. Minutes or hours after the call ends you get suspicious. Freed from the magic spell of their psychological thrall, you call your bank. And discover you have been robbed.

It is psychological warfare. So remember your weapon. Use that finger and end the call without a word of conversation.

ROMANCE FRAUD

More and more people find love and relationships online. But like the alleys round a nightclub (where we used to meet people), there are equally dark and dangerous places in cyber romance. You may have seen the Netflix true-crime drama *Tinder Swindler*. Criminals create fake profiles and lure unsuspecting people looking for love into a web of deceit. And when they have gained your trust or even what you think is their love, the requests for money begin. A staggering two out of every five people looking for love online have been asked for money. The requests can seem so reasonable. A train fare for a job interview. A flight home for a soldier. Cash flow problems in a business. All as loans, of course, which will be repaid in full – and more – on that magic day when I take you in my arms. In 2021, more than 25,000 people lost over £30 milllion to online romance fraud. Only £12 million was ever recovered.

Again, the protection is in your own hands. Never, ever, ever, give or lend money to someone you have only met online. Do not believe you can judge a character this way. And do not believe profiles or photos. If you are genuinely caught and feel you are somehow responsible for this person, ask your family or close real friends what to do. Don't be afraid or think they will say 'How could you be so stupid?' They are much more likely to say that after you have lost money. So ask them in good time before, rather than trusting someone you do not know and have never seen – and probably never will.

CONFIRMATION OF PAYEE

Whenever you pay someone new through your banking app or online, your bank may check if the account name you have put in, such as Vladimir Potansky, is actually the name on the account. This check does two things. First, it checks if you have mistyped the sort code or account number: 1324 8790 for 1243 8970, for example. Second, it checks the name. If the account is in fact owned by Jabberwock Holdings, it will say 'stop!' and give a red warning that the name is different from the name you entered. Or it will warn you that the numbers don't match. If you get such a warning, do not carry on with the payment. If you do, the bank may well say it has given you an adequate warning and will not reimburse you if Jabberwock Holdings turns out to be run by a thief. If it doesn't quite match, then it will give an amber warning and say the actual name is spelt in the Ukrainian way, Volodymir Potanski. It is up to you whether you proceed and think that is accurate. Or you can go back and spell it correctly. Then the bank will give you a big green tick and say details matched.

There are still some banks that are not in this system. If you try to move money to an account with one of them your bank will tell you that it is unable to check the name and you proceed at your own risk. Of course, the thieves know which banks these are and prefer to open accounts with them to avoid the check. If you get that message, it is a marker that this may be a theft. Do not proceed with the transfer unless you are 100 per cent certain of the details – they belong to a friend or colleague at work, for example, and they have personally told you the details. And that does not include telling you by a text or email that the details have changed. That could come from a thief. Find the individual's number and call them. Ask if there is another account you can pay it into.

Confirmation of payee only happens the first time you make a payment. After that, you will be free to send more money even if the name does not match. This huge loophole is exploited by thieves. The banks won't close it.

There is one simple change that could solve a lot of the problems. In some countries when you make an online payment to a new person or small business, the payment is automatically held for 24 hours. That gives time for you and your bank to consider the payment. Whenever I talk to victims of these crimes, they usually realise that something is wrong within hours, if not minutes. It would also stop you making a series of payments in a few hours. The government and the banks say they will not introduce this simple theft-prevention move.

CRM CODE

In May 2019, the major banks were forced to agree a Code that was supposed to ensure that innocent victims of this type of fraud would be reimbursed either by their own bank for allowing the payments to be made or by the bank the payment went to because it allowed thieves to open, operate and control an account. With their usual ability to invent new and meaningless jargon, they called it the Contingent Reimbursement Model (CRM) Code. It is 20 pages long and you can read it here **lendingstandardsboard.org.uk/crm-code**. Figures from the banks show that in 2021 less than half the money covered by the Code was actually returned to the customer.

The banks give various reasons for refusing. One is that they have given an effective warning, which was ignored. To me, the fact that the 'effective warning' did not prevent the crime means it was not effective! But the banks do not see it that way. They are also supposed to give special treatment to people who are vulnerable. In my experience, people tricked into letting the thieves steal their money are usually vulnerable, at least temporarily, and that is what the thieves exploit. Again, the banks take a different view. More recently, thieves – who adapt and change their techniques as the banks develop new systems to thwart them – have persuaded people to open a new account in their own name and then, because they are transferring money 'me to me', it is less likely to be flagged as a risk. But the new account is one the thieves can drain themselves. And they soon do.

CRYPTO CRIMINALS

Bitcoin or crypto assets are not an investment. They are a gamble at best and a fraud at worst. One bank told me that one in five transfers from its customers to a crypto-platform was part of a fraud. It has now banned all transfers by customers to crypto platforms. Other banks have not.

Investment fraud is rife. We are all fed up with low-interest rates on our cash savings. And this is exploited by thieves who offer better returns. Often they encourage you to transfer money to a safe investment, often abroad or, more likely nowadays, into a crypto asset. Once you start that process you are lost. As Graeme was. Settle down. It's a sad story. Graeme made a number of mistakes. But when you read them don't think what a fool. Think instead – I could have done that. And see how cleverly he is reeled in once he has taken the bait.

Graeme was 77 years old and an ex-RAF pilot, who had known war and personal tragedy. He was fed up with the low returns he was getting on his savings. He wanted to help one of his sons buy his first home. He had heard of bitcoin and other cryptoassets and thought he would try it to make higher returns. He googled 'bitcoin dealers'. That was Graeme's first mistake. Never, ever, ever google about investments. See page 206 in Investing for how to find free advice and top-quality paid-for advice.

And there were, on my count, fourteen other mistakes, including believing that an online account was genuine and showed his 'money'. They are easy to fake. When he was paid a 'return', it was just the return of some of his own money. He believed the big lie that his money was at risk (it was of course) and he had to send more money to recover it. This is the classic moment when greed for bigger returns is replaced by fear that you will lose it all. He then borrowed to send money. Never, ever, ever borrow to invest. He also trusted people he had never met and did what they suggested, even mortgaging then selling his own home. Never do anything under time pressure. The thieves literally bled Graeme dry of every penny he possessed, then disappeared. He lost £800,000.

Initially, both banks involved in transferring money refused to refund Graeme, though one did eventually admit some fault and return £28,000. The police are investigating. His family surrounded him with what they call a ring of steel made of love and practical help and told his story, hoping his experience will help others avoid the mistakes he made.

> ***'I would like you to pass on my thanks to Graeme and Liz for their courage and testimony on Saturday's* Money Box *episode. My 14-year-old son was with me, in the car, on our way back from his football match. He was***

> *touched by Graeme's story and in disbelief that anyone could be prepared to destroy someone's life like that and not care. There is no amount I could have said as a mum that would match Graeme's testimony and warning. So, thank you from the bottom of my heart.'*
>
> *Karine, via email*

For Graeme's sake and his family's, don't get caught as he did.

Remember

- Don't look for investment advice online. See page 206 on Investing. Investing isn't that difficult. And you can get some advice free.
- Don't trust firms that you have never heard of without checking carefully if they are regulated. If they are not, it is a fraud. As part of your check, see if they are clones of real firms. The Financial Conduct Authority (FCA) has a list of over 9500 unregulated firms that offer financial services illegally. Check at **fca.org.uk** and search 'unauthorised firms'.
- Don't believe an adviser who is new to you is your friend. They are not.
- Never borrow money to invest.
- Never chase your losses with more money. 'Throwing good money after bad' is a well-known phrase for a good reason.
- Never believe anyone who tells you that your money is at risk and they need more money to release it. That is always a lie.
- The government is considering whether it should make all banks subject to the CRM code and give it the force

of law. If it does, you can expect a lot of lobbying by the banks to include the various wheezes they use to refuse to pay their robbed customers.

IMPENETRABLE BARRIER

In case you have read this far and are still a bit like 'mmm it wouldn't fool me', here is a new way to behave. When you get a cold call or text or message, say to yourself:

> 'It's a lie. And the person saying it is a thief. It's a lie. And the person saying it is a thief. It's a lie. And the person saying it is a thief.'

It helps to say it out loud. This short invocation will build an impenetrable fortification around your online presence through which thieves cannot pass. They will come disguised as your bank brandishing its real helpline number. They will tell you that your money is at risk. But that is the only honest thing they will say. They will appear to know things about you that only your bank could know. Then when your guard is down, these zombies will leap forward and bleed your account to death.

It's a lie. And the person saying it is a thief. Repeat.

**IT'S A LIE.
AND THE PERSON
SAYING IT IS A THIEF.**

SPENDING 23–41

CHAPTER 6

Now onto sweeter things – though even they can turn sour! We've looked at work, taxes, benefits, auto-enrolment and debt. So what's left? Things you have to spend money on – your home, heating, insurance and, of course, the nice stuff – holidays, shopping and travelling about. This chapter explains how some of those things work and your rights when things go wrong. Armed with that knowledge, you can take on the financial world.

BUYING A HOME

I am prejudiced. After many years of hearing on *Money Box* about the problems faced by leaseholders, my firm advice is – if you can afford to buy a home, then buy a freehold house, which sits on a piece of land. The land and the building on it belong to you. Forever. There is nothing so secure. Of course, I know people have done that near the sea and ended up literally falling over a cliff. And some houses come with dry rot, leaky roofs, restrictive covenants, or appalling neighbours. But those are things to check before you buy. As for leasehold houses, forget it. They are a racket. So much so that the government has effectively banned developers from selling any more new-build leasehold houses. But there are still a lot of them around, which were sold in the past (see box below).

So, buy freehold whenever you can. I know it's not a choice everybody has. There are over four million leasehold properties in this country, often flats but including over a million houses. With a lease you get possession of a property but you don't own it. Leasehold usually means less expensive, but it can also mean nightmares for the buyers.

The problem with leasehold

With a leasehold you do not own the property, you just buy the right to live there for a period of time – usually 99 years, which seems forever but is not. The freeholder of a leasehold flat or house can then impose service charges on you (which they control), make you pay a ground rent (which can go up every few years), and impose restrictions on what you can do with your home – charging you for building a conservatory, for example.

Builders realised the potential of these sales in the 2010s and discovered they could not just sell you a home, they could sell the freehold on to investors whose only interest in you or your home is the stream of revenue it would produce. They could mire you in all sorts of legal difficulties if you tried to buy the freehold as the law says you can. As a result, these homes are hard to sell as lenders have now got cold feet about them and the price has fallen. After a damning report by the Competition and Markets Authority (CMA), new houses should not be sold in this way. And the CMA is now doing deals to remove the clauses that allow the freeholder to escalate the ground rents. Some firms have been forced to return them to their original price. But it is a slow process and my advice is still – if you can afford it, do not buy a leasehold house. But if you feel you have no choice, then read the rest of this section to be aware of the pitfalls.

Kath Williams told *Money Box* about her experience of buying a house on an estate in Cheshire:

> ***'I was misled and mis-sold. I bought the house in 2011 and there was no mention of leasehold anywhere. When I came to sell, the house was valued at £20,000 less than the freehold value and to buy the leasehold cost me £15,000.'***
>
> *Kath, via email*

As for a leasehold flat, all you buy is the right to live in 100 cubic metres of air enclosed by walls you don't own that stand on land you only rent. Like leasehold houses, that right will last only for a fixed number of years. So, every year that passes it is worth less. In addition, you will have regular outgoings for service charges that may or may not bring you any services, ground rent for which you get nothing at all, and maintenance obligations, which may cover the whole block not just your little bit of it. That alone can cost you tens of thousands of pounds that you were not expecting and may not have – and you are still at the mercy of the freeholder, the person or company who owns the fabric of the building and the land it sits on. You may also find that insurance and heating are controlled by the freeholder, so you have no choice but to pay what they demand.

After a lot of complaints – including on *Money Box* – some big housebuilders have now started solving these problems for new-build homes. Historically, not only does the freeholder own the ground on which the building stands, they can also charge leaseholders what is called 'ground rent'. Yes, you pay rent for the ground under your home. Ground rent for all new leasehold contracts signed from 30 June 2022 or later has been fixed at zero (except for retirement homes, where the change comes in April 2023). The Competition and Markets Authority has been very active in persuading builders and ground rent speculators to stop unfair practices. Leases on new-builds are now longer – as long as 999 years in some cases – and in some cases, the management of the block of flats is being given to the leaseholders from the start. But we still do not know how these changes will spread.

> ***'Six months after accepting an offer on our flat, the bank has today withdrawn their mortgage offer due to doubling ground rent every 21 years. Feared it might happen but such a kick in the teeth.'***
>
> *Charlotte, via Twitter*

If you feel you must buy a leasehold property, these are the questions to ask:

- What happens when the lease comes to an end? Can I extend the lease? (Yes, but it's usually expensive.) The Leasehold Advisory Service's (LAS) lease extension calculator gives you a guide to the costs of extending the lease of a flat. See **lease-advice.org**.
- Can I buy the freehold? (Sometimes, but again it may be costly. Far better to buy a flat where the previous owner has done this for you.)

- What are the service charges? (In addition to the lease, there may be a charge for the maintenance of communal areas. That may include insurance, which may involve still more price hikes. And it may include communal heating systems, where the flats in the block all pay a share of the cost of the gas the communal boiler uses.)
- If it is not a new property, what is the ground rent and how does it increase?

You should ask those questions of your own solicitor who you found independently. Never use a solicitor recommended by a developer or builder, who will probably have a conflict of interest.

It is best to look for a property advertised with 'a share of the freehold.' The array of costs will still be there but at least you get a say in how the money is spent.

Cladding and maintenance

Since the devastating fire at Grenfell Tower in west London, which killed 72 people, hundreds of blocks of flats have become unsellable money pits for the unfortunate leaseholders. The problems are slowly being solved, but the essential problem with leasehold flats is that if the block needs refurbishment, roof repairs, window replacement or even just painting, all leaseholders will be expected to pay a share – including the cost of scaffolding the whole building. These costs can run into tens of thousands of pounds.

So, until the feudal system of leasehold is finally abolished and replaced with what is normal in most other countries – often called commonhold – my advice remains: if you can possibly avoid it, do not buy leasehold.

Scottish note

If you live in Scotland you are lucky. And not just because of the open roads and lots of lovely views. In Scotland 'freehold' is normally called 'heritable title'. And as for leasehold, it was largely abolished in 2012. In Scotland, you need a solicitor when you buy a home and can discuss with them the legal position, including any restrictions on the property you want to buy.

Mortgages

Most people who buy a home – especially their first home – borrow the money to do so. It is called a mortgage and it is different from other forms of debt. First, it is probably fairly cheap borrowing. You can be paying as little as 3% interest as I write, though that is rising. Secondly, it is secured. That means if you don't pay it, the firm that lent you the money can forcibly sell your home to recover what you owe. That very seldom happens but sometimes it does. Meeting your mortgage payments is the single most important debt you have, so always pay it as a priority.

If you need a mortgage you should be prepared!

The deposit

Nowadays lenders will want a big deposit. Here are the basics to keep in mind:

- The very minimum is 5% of the sale price and with the average home costing around £275,000, that is still a chunk of cash – £13,750 in fact.

- First-time buyers might pay on average £50,000 less and the average hides a very wide range in different parts of the UK.
- Bigger deposits may be demanded, especially for the best deals.
- You may be able to borrow up to five times your income – or five times you and your partner's combined income.

As I write, the mortgage market is in some turmoil with offers being withdrawn as the markets fear big interest rate rises into 2023. But here is a key rule that won't change. You will always find that the bigger the deposit, the lower the interest rate. So, you should find the biggest deposit you can lay your hands on. By paying more upfront, you borrow less, and that money you do borrow is charged at a lower rate. Win-win.

As rates are so volatile, I won't set out the arithmetic, which would be hopelessly out of date by the time you read this. But it will always be true that a bigger deposit will keep your monthly payment down, hopefully to something you can afford and can save you hundreds – even thousands – of pounds a year in repayments. I presume you have your mum's phone number to hand?

Check the current situation at the national whole of market broker **landc.co.uk**. It has calculators so you can look at the current cost of borrowing under various scenarios.

Get the best deal

The cheapest deals normally fix your rate for two or more years. That means in two years' time you will be moved to what is called the lender's standard variable rate or SVR. That is likely to be a lot higher than the deal you got. That would, of course, whoosh your monthly payments up to perhaps twice what they are now. At that point, most people try to get another fixed-rate deal by finding another firm to lend them the money they still owe – which, after two years, will be pretty much the same because most of the early payments are interest. Fourteen years ago, interest rates were 6% and some mortgage deals are already that high. With inflation rising strongly and interest rates going up, the repayments may well be higher on your next loan.

As I write, there are around 4000 different mortgage products to choose from. No human can choose rationally between more than half a dozen things. So, we have to rely on brokers – people who sit between us and the lender and find the best deal for us. But brokers are human too and, like us, can't hold more than six or seven things in their head at once. So they use algorithms, which they feed with your details and desires and it churns out recommendations. The broker will then pare these down to half a dozen and talk you through them.

Two- or three-year fixed rates are normally recommended. Not least because a broker who recommends that knows you will be back for more in a couple of years' time. If they sell you a long-term variable rate mortgage, you may not be back for 25 years. So always remember the broker has a conflict of interest. That is why it is a good idea to go to a broker that is what is called 'whole of market'. They will look at every one of those 4000 mortgages and find the number one for you. Also, it is better to find a big national chain that is not here today and gone tomorrow. Never ask your bank. They cannot find you the best deal.

Be good

And speaking of banks, there are important steps to take while you prepare to buy that first home. In the past, lenders would simply multiply your salary by 3.5 and say that is what we will lend you. Nowadays, it is much more complicated. You may be able to borrow up to five times your gross pay – time, like house prices, has moved on! But the regulator – the Financial Conduct Authority – makes them assess the affordability of the loan. They check if you are a good person to lend to who will not default on the mortgage and put them to all the trouble and bad publicity of throwing you out and auctioning off your house. They check affordability in several ways.

First, they will do a credit check. These are explained in detail in Chapter 4 on page 72 but the basics are:

- get on the electoral register
- don't move often
- have a credit card with a decent credit limit but never spend more than half of it
- never, ever, ever make a payment late or not at all – ever

Second, they will want to nosey around in what you spend your money on. Most of us spend to our income. OK, we might save a bit but basically, if we get a pay rise, we enjoy ourselves a bit more. Not if you want to be a homebuyer, you don't! For a year before you apply for the mortgage, do not have an overdraft, make sure money coming in is more than money going out. Cut back on meals out, drinks, expensive holidays. Pretend it's still Covid time! Your bank will want to see statements to prove all this. So make sure that when it looks at them it is clear you can readily afford the monthly repayments.

In fact, it will go further. When assessing if you can afford your mortgage, the lender will not just check if you can afford your current deal, it will also check if you could afford the mortgage repayments if interest rates rose by at least 1%. It could use a higher figure if it expects interest rates to rise by more than that.

So, don't just spend your time saving for a deposit. Watch your spending. Become the perfect borrower.

Value or price?

The value of a home is what someone will pay for it on the day you want to sell it. Neither more nor less. So, if you already have a home do not worry about whether it has gone up in value or down. It is still worth one house, or flat or bungalow. The only time that price is a concern is if it has fallen and you borrowed more than your home is now worth. That is called 'negative equity' because if you subtract your debt from the value of your home, you get a minus number. Even that does not matter unless you have to move – for a job or an up- or down-size, or after a relationship ends. Because when you sell, your lender will have to be paid back more than your home is worth. So negative equity can trap you in a home until its price rises again.

SHARED OWNERSHIP

I am sorry to say I keep shared ownership in my 'don't-do-it-if-you-can-possibly-avoid-it' box. As house prices have risen to unaffordable levels, new ways have been invented to try to keep homes affordable. Shared ownership is one. It is often marketed as a way to take that first step on the housing ladder or some such nonsense (there isn't a ladder). And it may be. But for many it is not.

The property is built by the local housing association. It will allocate some to shared ownership. That means you buy a proportion of it and rent the rest. So you buy between 10 per cent and 75 per cent of the value of the home and pay rent for the rest of it. Not all lenders will provide a mortgage for them and the rates they charge may be more than the best you can get when you don't share the ownership with a landlord. When you add up the rent and the mortgage repayments, you may not have saved very much at all. The hope is that you will 'staircase' up (notice the ladder has gone) and buy another share and another until you own it all. The evidence is, though, that very few people ever staircase to buy 100 per cent of a shared ownership property. And even when they do, they are all leasehold properties anyway – see page 138 for my thoughts on that! At the very best, it means there will be annual charges to pay. And unlike some other leaseholds, you will never be able to buy the freehold. It also may be hard to sell, especially for the price you paid, and the housing association you bought it from will still have a say in who can buy it. So avoid it if you can. If you feel it is for you, then do the arithmetic and check carefully what the costs of full leasehold ownership will be, including all those pesky extras like 'service charges', and what price you may be able to sell it for – ask local estate agents.

In 2021 – it seems a long time ago now! – there was a studio flat on Floor 13 of a London tower. Its 'full value' was given as £555,000 but you could buy a quarter of it for £138,750 if you had a £6938 deposit. It is about 50 square metres. One room to sleep in, one to live and cook in, and one to ablute in. What does that feel like or look like? What is the ceiling height? Is there wall space to put things on? You will not know because you will not see it until you have bought it and it has been built (in that order), for this is an off-plan purchase. In other words, you buy it from an approximate drawing in a brochure. It will cost you £1539 a month, consisting of £691 for the mortgage to buy a quarter of it and £607 to rent the rest. That comes to £1298 a month and the remaining £241 is a service charge for a 24/7 concierge and access to a communal garden. If you want to use the gym, viewing platform, residents lounge, private cinema, media room or golf simulator, they are extra – once they are built. And if you do find another £416,250 to buy the other 75 per cent of your home, those charges will continue. They are uncapped and unregulated.

But it is a half-million-pound apartment in London, not far from all those offices where people used to work. All for less than £1298 a month (plus charges). So, I can see the temptation.

Outside cities, most shared ownership homes are in fact houses. For them, shared ownership can work well. When *Money Box* looked at shared ownership recently, the majority of listeners with positive stories had used it as a way to buy a freehold house, not a flat.

RENTING

Renting is a good option for many people. Sure, it does not give you the ultimate security of owning a bit of land and a house built on it. But renting is good for flexible living, for moving on and, in some cases, it is all that people can afford. Young people often think it is their only choice and for many it may be. In some other countries – Germany is often held up as the example – renting is simply the normal way to live.

The big problem about renting in England and Wales is that as a tenant you have almost no rights. Even if you pay your rent on time, keep the place clean and tidy and don't have noisy parties every night, your landlord can evict you without a reason and normally at just two months' notice.

Of course, most landlords do not do that and are good to their tenants. But because the possibility of being told to go even exists, a rented place cannot feel like a home to put down roots and, if you are so minded, bring up children. The previous government but one published plans to change the law in England so a landlord cannot evict tenants for no reason. However, those plans do give a range of reasons for a forced eviction – including the landlord wanting to sell or live there themselves, as well as serious rent arrears. Rent increases will only be allowed once a year with two months' notice and tenants can challenge unreasonable increases at a tribunal. A new private renting ombudsman will be created. It is not known when these changes will begin or whether the third Conservative Prime Minister in as many months will take them forward. In Scotland, where laws are often more sensible, tenants already have more rights and are protected from random evictions. In Wales and Northern Ireland, the law is also changing to give tenants more notice.

Deposit

When you agree to rent a property you will be asked for a deposit. In England and Wales this cannot be more than four weeks' rent. Throughout the UK, it has to be held in an approved tenancy deposit scheme (TDP) and your landlord must tell you in writing where that is. If they do not, they are breaking the law and can be forced to pay you money. When you move out, there is often a dispute about the state of the place. The landlord may demand money to redecorate or replace carpets or make good damage. They will use money from your deposit for that. You can apply for the return of your deposit and challenge that decision. All that should be made clear when you first move in. See **gov.uk** or **mygov.scot** or **nidirect.gov.uk** and search 'tenancy deposit'.

Remember

- If you can, try to buy a freehold home.
- If you can't do that, then take great care over the charges you face for a leasehold home and remember that as years pass by, the lease is worth less and less.
- Think carefully about your mortgage – get the biggest deposit you can and keep your finances in very good order for a year before you apply.
- If you rent, be aware of your rights as a tenant.

THE ENERGY CRISIS

As I write this section, the domestic energy market in England, Scotland and Wales is broken. By that, I mean the way we pay for the electricity and gas wired and piped into our homes. It finally broke in the autumn of 2021, though the warning signs had been there for years. It will still be broken by the time you read this, even if we are by then into a second edition.

In my first draft of this book, I had a long section explaining how it was failing and how changing supplier every year or two could mean paying a little less at the expense of people who didn't. The result was complexification into tens of thousands of tariffs, which no-one could rationally compare, and inevitably many ended up overpaying. None of this endless 'switching' reduced the fundamental price of electricity or gas – probably the opposite. But it gave personal finance journalists a lot to write about, the government much to trumpet, and £60 to the online comparison websites every time someone 'switched' from one supplier to another in the pursuit of a few pounds off a bill that would nowadays look ludicrously low.

The market was false anyway because energy suppliers do not supply us with electricity or gas. They just bill us for it at the price they offer. The supply comes from the National Grid through the wires and pipes of the local network operator. And switch as we might, that did not change. If a supplier failed, then the supply was guaranteed and the customer was forcibly 'switched' to be billed by another supplier. Without that promise, few would have risked changing.

Because of the exploitative behaviour of energy suppliers in the past, the regulator Ofgem was forced by the government to set a price cap. No supplier could charge more for electricity or gas than the cap. But time lags in the Ofgem bureaucracy meant that the cap that began in the autumn of 2021 was below the actual cost and the new cap in April 2022 – even though it was an average 81% higher for gas units and 36% for electricity units – was even further below. Only the biggest firms could survive. Nearly 30 went bust taking customer money with them. Big firms took over the two million customers affected and the cost of that is spread among all other bill payers at a cost of £94 each.

The cap only applied to what is called the 'standard variable tariff'. Firms were allowed to offer fixed-rate deals above the price cap, but they were vastly more expensive so no-one wanted them. As a result, the cap was the price just about all of us paid. Or rather, the prices we all paid – Ofgem had 252 separate caps defined by:

- region (14)
- fuel (2)
- payment method (3)
- unit cost or standing charge (2)
- electricity by day or night use (2)

Then in September 2022, faced with a massive rise in the price cap from October, the Government replaced the cap with an Energy Price Guarantee that fixed the cost of every unit of electricity and gas we used. That price, fixed from 1 October 2022, will last until the end of March 2023. However, it keeps the complex Ofgem structure, so the actual price per unit varies from region to region and by different payment methods. After March there will almost certainly be a new scheme but it is not clear who will be helped or by how much.

I explained this structure to one listener who contacted me:

> ***'Dear Paul, thank you yet again for all that information; as you say, it is all so complicated and hard to understand.***
>
> ***Best, Graham'***
>
> ***Graham, via email***

So today, just as Stalin told Russians the price of bread in the 1950s, the government tells us the price of electricity and gas. At least until March 2023. As I write the plans of the latest government for a scheme from April 2023 have not been published. There is no competition and the market is broken. In Northern Ireland, there was no price cap but the government has given a discount off the unit price of gas and electricity which it says gives households the same amount of financial help.

A scheme began in October 2022 to reduce electricity bills still further. From October to March 2023 electricity bills in England, Scotland and Wales will be reduced by £66 or £67 a month. Similar help is being given to households in Northern Ireland.

Billing type

Although the false market in electricity and gas has gone, the remnants remain. There are three ways to pay your bill:

- estimated amounts by monthly direct debit
- accurate amounts by prepayment meter
- accurate amounts by quarterly billing

Estimated monthly direct debit

This is the cheapest and allows the firms to build up credit balances, which they can use to help with their cash flow or investment – even though they should not do so. Monthly payment is sold to customers as (a) cheaper and (b) fits in with their monthly wages or benefit payments. Suppliers will now let you pay for exactly what you use each month if you have a smart meter or send it monthly meter readings. Ask yours for details if that would suit you.

Prepayment meters

These meters now charge very slightly less per unit than monthly direct debit tariffs but a lot more for the standing charge, so overall prepayment customers pay more for their energy – and the less they use, the more that price difference grows. Typically, at October 2022 prices, they pay £58 a year more.

Quarterly billing

This is the most expensive way to pay. Both the standing charge and the unit rate are higher and typically energy bills are £159 a year more just because of the way you pay. The same charges apply whether you pay quarterly by cheque, credit card or direct debit.

If you can switch to monthly, you will save money. If you build up a credit balance, you have the right to ask for it back. But your direct debit may then be raised. If you think your direct debit is too high, ask for it to be reduced. Or tell your bank to stop authorising it until you and the firm agree a fair price. Or tell your supplier you want to pay just for what you use. The risk of being difficult is you may be moved to prepayment. If you have a smart meter, that can be done remotely. Then you will pay more and have the hassle of topping it up.

Cut down on costs

When you use electricity to heat up anything – whether it is your home, water or an iron – that takes a lot of energy. If you want to boil water, a pan on a gas hob is cheaper, even though it is not very efficient (heat leaks out the sides), because a unit of electricity costs more than three times as much as a unit of gas. A unit is a kilowatt-hour or kWh and it is a measure of energy used per hour.

- Only fill the kettle with what you need for the hot drink you are making.
- Take shorter showers and shallower – or indeed shared – baths.
- Use the dishwasher only when it is full.
- Never use the tumble dryer if there is an alternative – like sunshine or a drying rack – but if your flat or house is damp that can make it worse.

No-one really struggling with paying their bills needs to be told this. They have worked it out already. But with the numbers of those in fuel poverty growing rapidly, a new section of society suddenly has to find ways to reduce what they use.

One common suggestion is to turn the heating thermostat down by 1°. That will save you money. At least it will the first time. After 20 years when your thermostat is at zero, you may find you have hypothermia! Seriously, cold kills especially as you get older. So do not be cold to save money.

Standing charge

We pay twice for our electricity and gas. We pay for the units of energy we use – measured in kilowatt-hours or kWh and those are what we can try to cut down. But before a sniff of gas or a spark of electricity arrives, we pay a standing charge – a fee just to be connected. This standing charge depends on how you pay and, for electricity, which of the 14 regions you live in. The average standing charge for electricity from October 2022 is £169 a year for direct debit but £187 a year for prepayment and £191 for quarterly payment. Gas is less but still £104, £137 or £122 a year. Of course, we cannot reduce this charge by wearing more layers or washing in cold water. Someone on a prepayment meter with electricity and gas will pay an average of £6.24 a week even when they have run out of money and are sitting in the cold and dark.

Originally the standing charge was the cost of the pipes and wires and the administration costs of having you as a customer. Rather as if Sainsbury's added a fee at the till for the cost of its lorry fleet and rent. But now the electricity standing charge has had other costs loaded onto it, including the cost of those failed suppliers and the extra cost of green initiatives.

Smart meters

I have never been a fan of smart meters. The first generation of them was not very smart at all and if you switched supplier, they went dumb and had to be read by a human, which was often difficult as they were not designed for it. Four million of the smart meters already fitted are still working in dumb mode. The second generation – called SMETS 2 – do not have that fault and the in-home displays (see box below) are useful when we want to save energy. And – see page 27 in Chapter 2 – they can be used to teach children, as well as adults, the cost of using electricity. So if you are offered a smart meter there is no reason not to accept it, although it does give the energy supplier a lot of information about you and, in the future, the ability to interfere in your energy use (see box below). When they work …

> ***'Just wanted to let you know after your tweet about any smart meters/home display units not working and my reply about mine not working. Energy supplier DM'd me and I had all of them replaced. All working now, great service! Thank you.'***
>
> ***Liz, via Twitter***

What is a smart meter?

Smart meters don't just measure the flow of gas and electricity into your home. They also report how much energy you are using back to the energy supplier through a national communications network – which cost £4 billion. So your meter never has to be read by anyone popping round to the house when you are out and leaving a card saying 'sorry I missed you'. That means, in theory, that accurate bills can be sent to you every month. However, some firms still prefer to send you estimated bills averaged out over the year. You can change to accurate monthly bills if you want to.

Smart meters also tell you how much energy you are using in real time through what is called an in-home display (IHD) and what it is costing you. So you can see that the kettle and the washing machine use a lot of electricity but a modern TV uses very little. One fun thing to try if you have an IHD is to see if you can get electricity use down to zero. I bet you can't! So much is on standby or virtually unswitchoffable that electricity is leaking away just keeping the devices we all depend on ready to jump to our every whim. Watching the money slip away is supposed to make us more efficient in our use of energy. And that will save us money.

However, only a third of the theoretical savings from smart meters are made by consumers cutting down on their energy use. Half the savings are made by the energy suppliers and networks, partly by sacking all the meter readers and partly by being able to switch us to a prepayment meter remotely. We just do not know if (a) they really will make savings and (b) whether they will pass them on to us if they do. I would guess 'maybe eventually' and 'no' are the answers. Although 50 per cent of the savings are expected to be made by the energy companies, 100 per cent of the cost of fitting them in every home will be met – in fact is being met – by us through higher bills. £19 a year on the latest estimate.

Smart meters also allow for what is called 'time of use' tariffs. So it would cost less to charge your car or run the tumble dryer at night. But it also means that your energy provider could charge more to cook breakfast at breakfast time and less at eleven in the morning when you are at school or work. In the future, a new generation of smart devices will allow the supplier to turn them on and off remotely if you are using power at the 'wrong' time.

One final warning. A lot of people tell me that the IHD, or indeed the smart meter itself, does not work properly and it is difficult, if not impossible, to get the supplier to replace them.

Smart meters are not being fitted in Northern Ireland.

Oil and LPG

Although almost everyone has an electricity supply, about five million households in high-rise flats, rural areas and most of Northern Ireland do not have piped gas. Many in rural areas and NI rely on tanks of heating oil or liquefied petroleum gas (LPG), either in a tank or bottles. These fuels are not regulated. As prices on world markets have soared, the market has ruled and prices have doubled or more. Customers are in a time-slot lottery hoping their empty tank will not coincide with a market price peak. The government has promised a payment of £100 for people who heat their home this way. It will be paid by a credit on electricity bills.

WATER

Thankfully, you cannot switch water supplier. You are stuck with the one that pipes it to your address. Your only choice is to pay a flat charge per year or have a meter fitted and pay for what you use. The fewer people in the house, the more likely a meter will save you money. One rule of thumb is that if there are more bedrooms than people, a meter might save you money. Or in England and Wales try this calculator – **ccwater.org.uk/watermetercalculator**. In some areas, meters are becoming compulsory. In others, you can choose to have one and, if you don't save money, you can switch back to a flat charge. If a house has been converted to separate flats it may be more difficult to have a meter. The water company will have to find the stopcock to turn off water to each flat. That may be hidden behind fitted kitchens and bathrooms. Contact your local water supplier that bills you. If you find it hard to pay your bill all water companies offer 'social tariffs' to people who need them which should save you money. In Scotland, all water is supplied by Scottish Water and charges depend on your council tax band. You can choose to have a meter but you pay for its installation. In Northern Ireland, there are no domestic water charges.

INSURANCE

I am not a fan of insurance. Some of it you must have – some you should have – but much of it is a waste of money. In response to frequent stories about insurance not paying up, I usually tweet:

Insurance gives you peace of mind – until you claim.

> ***'We paid almost £2K pa for 'All Risks' comprehensive buildings and contents insurance. Thieves removed £1000 lead roof! Claim rejected because "theft of building fabric" not covered by building or contents cover!!!'***
>
> ***Peter (who runs a local scout group), via Twitter***

> ***'Suffered flood damage last year. The insurance company are still refusing to acknowledge that it was a flood and are repudiating our claim. It is scandalous.'***
>
> ***Ross, via Twitter***

Of course, most claims are met quickly without fuss and both sides are happy. But some are not and they are the ones who write to me. So I may be biased.

What insurance do you need?

- **Car insurance.** Yes, it's the law. Ditto motorbikes.
- **Home building insurance.** If you have a mortgage, yes. If you don't, it is almost always a good idea.
- **Home contents insurance.** Generally, yes. But it does depend on how much stuff you have.
- **Life insurance.** Yes, but only if (a) you have a mortgage jointly with a partner (take out life insurance on each of you that is just enough to cover the outstanding loan) or (b) if you have children or other financial dependants (but only until they stop being dependent). It's called term insurance and it is good value, though about one in thirty claims is refused, the insurance trade body the ABI says.
- **Critical illness.** Pays out if you are diagnosed with one of a list of named serious illnesses. Renowned for the illnesses and conditions it did not cover. One in 11 claims is refused. Total permanent disability has an even worse record – refusing one in 3 claims.
- **Income protection.** Replaces some or all of your income for a while if you lose your job for specified reasons. One in 7 claims refused.
- **Travel insurance.** Probably, especially now we are out of the EU, though there will still be some protection there for health costs on holiday. Make sure the insurance covers medical costs and the activity you are going to do – research in a library is cheap, naked paragliding over the Rocky Mountains

will not be – and where you are going – the USA charges the most for medical bills, so insurance for travel there is the most expensive.

- **Pet insurance.** Maybe, because vet bills are crazy prices but then so is pet insurance and may itself fuel the price rises. Call me cruel and horrible, but there comes a time when a pet animal has to be allowed to die peacefully.
- **Health insurance.** No. It gets more expensive as you get older and the chances of needing it grow. If you need private medical care to bypass an NHS queue, then pay for it at the time. Remember, the price of the health insurance assumes you will get all your medical needs privately. Few people do.
- **Legal insurance.** This is sold as an add-on to motor or home insurance. Often both. It is not expensive. But will it really help in that once-in-a-lifetime dispute with your ex-partner's son over who owns the Winnebago?
- **Wedding insurance.** No. Have a cheap wedding and save yourself thousands of pounds. It can be done for £200.
- **Mobile phone insurance.** No. Whenever I write this people contact me saying it saved me a fortune on all three occasions I was drunk and dropped my phone down the toilet – oh no, wait, once was over a harbour wall. I was having a pee but it wasn't a toilet, as such. I sigh and shake my head.
- **Payment protection insurance.** No. The banks have paid out more than £40 billion for mis-selling it.

- **Funeral insurance.** Never. If your total assets are around £3000 or more, then your relatives can pay out of your estate. If they are less, you probably should not spend the money on it. Go out and enjoy yourself instead.
- **Extended warranty (which is a kind of insurance).** No. Use your consumer rights if things go wrong. The chances of faults after that and during the warranty are low.
- **Breakdown cover.** Yes, if you have an old vehicle or one that is likely to breakdown.
- **Business insurance and professional indemnity insurance.** Maybe, or even probably, but this book is not about business.
- **Any insurance sold as part of buying something.** No. For example, when you buy a car and are offered tyre insurance, gap insurance, sun roof insurance, smile and say no thanks. And while I am here, is there anything you do on the price of the car?

More on the ones you need:

Car insurance

If you have a car or van or motorbike, it must be insured. It is a legal requirement. That is because if your vehicle hits a person or another vehicle, the damage it can do is huge and putting it right can cost massive amounts of money. The most costly of all is injuring another person so that their lives are changed – they may need care or medical treatment for years or even for life. That can cost millions of pounds, way beyond the resources of any individual. So you have insurance to pay those costs. Much of the premium you pay is for the tiny risk that you might be in such an accident. That is why whether your car is brand new and costs £20,000 or an old banger that costs a few hundred, the insurance may not be very different. It is not the cost of replacing your vehicle you are insuring against. It is the cost of the life-changing injuries you can inflict on someone else.

That is why the cost of insuring depends so much on your age. When you are young and reckless you are more likely to have an expensive accident. When you are old and your reactions slow down, your risk also goes up. But in the middle there is a sweet spot – around age 40 – where your risk is at its lowest. Of course, these are all averages and some young people are models of care and sobriety and some middle-aged folk are impatient know-it-alls who really should not be on the road at all.

These averages over millions of customers over billions of miles mean that insurers know pretty much the chance of an individual of a certain age having an accident and what it will cost.

So why, you ask, are the premiums so different from one firm to the next? That is simply because insurance is nothing more nor less than gambling. The insurance company takes your premium and bets with itself that over the next year it will collect more in premiums than it will pay out in claims.

The premiums are decided by people called actuaries. They are good at sums – especially those that no human really has a natural feel for called statistics. Which basically means assessing the chance of something happening. Each insurer has its own actuaries and each of them takes their own view about risk and analyses the millions of bits of data from past accidents differently. So some firms are better for the very young. Some better for people who are home owners. Some firms will not insure journalists. They cut up the data in different ways and decide how best they can make a profit. That is why moving across a postcode border can affect your premium. Or adding your new husband to your policy. It is just statistics. It can also help to pick the best job title when you have a choice or to offer to pay more 'excess' – the amount you pay of any claim. But beware – there will be a built-in compulsory excess – say £250. If you then offer to pay a voluntary excess of £500, you will pay the first £750 of any claim. There is a good guide to saving money on insurance at **which.co.uk** – search 'car and home insurance'.

Your home

If you own your own home, you should insure the building. If you have a mortgage, then the lender will insist on it. That does not mean you have to take the insurance they offer. As with any financial product, you should look at what is on offer and pick the best for you. One problem is over-insurance. If you insure your building then you are paying for the not uncommon event of a high wind taking off a couple of roof tiles. Or perhaps rain getting in and damaging your paintwork or flooring. But the real thing you are insuring against is catastrophic loss. A fire or flood or just a freak lightning bolt damaging your home so severely it has to be rebuilt. In many parts of the country, the rebuilding cost is actually a lot less than what you paid for it. So make sure you insure for that, not the inflated price you were silly enough to buy it for.

Your possessions

The contents of your home are also worth insuring. You would be surprised how much the furniture and clothes and electronic devices would cost to replace if a natural disaster, or indeed a burglar, did strike. Nowadays many insurers just say they will cover everything and the premium is based on the number of bedrooms rather than writing down all the things that you love. But make sure that those special things are covered. Furniture that is not antique should be 'new for old', in other words you get that six-year-old sofa the cat occasionally pees on replaced with a new one. Jewellery should be like-for-like replacements. So if your £1000 engagement ring is nicked or falls down the plughole, make sure you can replace it with something that is identical. Many insurers do a deal with a high-street chain and you will get a voucher saying 'one engagement ring' on it. To fight this, take pictures – go on do it now – and demand a like-for-like replacement. That is especially important if you have some precious family jewellery that grandma once wore. Never accept a Ratners voucher (I know it no longer exists, but if I mentioned one that did I could be sued). You want the jewel replaced with something old and similar worth the same or with an exact modern copy. Or just take the valuation money and go and replace it yourself.

Excess

With most insurance products you pay the first amount of the claim. That may be the first £100. If you volunteer to pay a higher excess, then the premiums will be lower. That means the insurer is not bothered with small claims that are not worth making. If you can afford it, pick a higher excess and cut your premiums. But beware you read the small print, as Andy warned me in a tweet. He was staying in a holiday villa with his family. He had a £150 excess but ended up paying the first £600 of the cost when he got burgled in Portugal a few years back:

> ***'Our policy had a £150 excess but they refused to pay us out as the excess was per person on the policy. There were four of us – two adults and two***

children both under ten. Even if every item stolen had belonged to me, it was still four x the excess.'

Andy, via Twitter

So, always check the small print!

Tricks of the trade

Insurers have some nasty tricks up their sleeve. Auto-renewal means that once you have given an insurance company your credit or debit card details, it is free to charge you for the insurance again next year unless you cancel it (technically you have to agree to this but you will not notice it happening). Until January 2022 when the regulator stepped in, insurers could not resist putting up the price. And year after year the price charged to loyal customers slowly went up until, like a frog in a pan of water on the stove, people eventually realised they were being boiled alive.

Since that major rule change, insurers cannot charge existing customers more than they charge new customers. So, of course, all premiums were put up!

But it is still a good idea to never, ever, ever accept a renewal premium. Go onto a comparison website. Get a better deal – you may even get one with your existing insurer – and then call your insurance company and ask for a reduction. If you do not get one, then transfer to the cheaper insurer.

Do not call:

'Hello. I have my car insurance with you and I had a small bump in the car park – not my fault at all – but I just wondered if I claim will my no-claims bonus be cut?'

Just by making that call, you have already put your premium up for next year. You have admitted a scrape and the actuaries will put a big 'likely to have another accident' sign by your name. So, never, ever make this call. The only times to call your insurer are when you want to make a claim or, of course, you need to amend a policy to add or subtract a person or change a vehicle, or renew it.

Loss adjusters

Like actuaries, loss adjusters are there to make money for the insurer. The moment you make a claim, the loss adjusters will swing into action to see how to get you to accept less than you should be paid. If it is a really big claim, then it is worth hiring your own expert – called a loss assessor. Let them argue the toss over what you can and cannot claim for and hopefully save you more than their fee.

As with so many financial products, we normally turn to online comparison websites when we pick a premium. This race to the bottom can be good of course. And it has certainly increased competition and reduced prices. But it is vital that you make sure you are comparing like-for-like products. Put in exactly the same details and ask yourself if you really need that courtesy Bentley while yours is off the road after an accident.

One thing that is essential and I know you wouldn't do it but ... never, ever, ever lie or fail to tell the truth when asked a question on an insurance application. It will invalidate any claim and all your premiums will have been wasted. Ker-chingggg!

SPENDING FOR FUN!

Pay by card

The best way to buy things is to use a credit card. It gives you extra consumer protection. But even with a debit card, you should be able to claim your money back from your bank if things go wrong.

If you use a credit card to buy anything – from a holiday to a sofa, the latest electronic gizmo to designer gear – the bank (all credit-card providers are banks) is equally liable with the retailer if what you buy goes wrong. **The only rule is that the item must cost more than £100** (and no more than £30,000 but that won't happen often!).

For example, you pay on a credit card for a flight that is cancelled. Or you buy expensive cosmetics online but they never arrive. Or you cannot resist ordering that drone but it never takes off. Or you take out a subscription for seeds that is actually a fraud. In all those cases, you can use your legal right to get your money back from your credit card provider.

That is because when you pay with a credit card, the bank that provides it has what is called 'joint liability' for the goods. That means the bank and the supplier are equally liable if things go wrong. This handy law is nearly 50 years old and is called **section 75 protection** or just **s.75** after the part of the Consumer Credit Act 1974 that originally gave you these rights.

It applies even if you just pay part of the cost on the credit card. Perhaps you pay a £50 deposit on a £350 wardrobe and the rest by bank transfer. If the wardrobe does not arrive or is broken or not the finish you ordered, the credit card provider has to refund you for the whole cost. If goods are sent to you but fail to arrive, then the supplier is liable until they are safely delivered to you. And so is the bank. If the goods are not exactly what you ordered or they are broken or they go wrong in a few months, then ask for your money back.

Normally, of course, you will go to the supplier first and deal with them. Or if it is travel, you might have insurance. But if the supplier is abroad or refuses to answer or has gone bust or the insurer refuses to pay, then go to your credit card provider and start a s.75 claim. It is not a fallback position. The bank is just as liable as the retailer. If a holiday insurance company is being difficult, then put in a s.75 claim to your bank. If it responds by saying you must do more to try to get your money back, then remind the bank that it has joint liability under s.75 of the Consumer Credit Act 1974. If the bank is difficult about it – and some have been recently, especially over some types of fraud – threaten to go to the Financial Ombudsman Service. You can do that if a dispute is not resolved in eight weeks. It would cost the bank £750 win or lose. So they may just pay up.

There is no time limit on a s.75 claim but obviously it is best to do it as soon as you can. If you leave it more than six years, you may find that any claim is time-barred under general laws.

Chargeback

There is a second right you have that applies when you pay with a debit card, a pre-paid card or a credit card. It is called chargeback and gives you very similar rights to s.75 and allows you to ask your bank to reverse the transaction on a credit or debit card if something has gone wrong. There is no minimum £100 spend – though Mastercard will not accept claims under a tenner – so it can be useful with a credit card if you spent £100 or less. Some people will tell you chargeback is not a 'legal right' as s.75 is. That is sort of true but also sort of misleading. It is a binding right because it is part of the contract between banks and the three payment networks – Visa, Mastercard and American Express.

You make the chargeback claim to whoever provides your card. That bank then claims the money back from the bank the supplier uses. That bank should pay your bank but usually it will first ask the supplier for the funds. If the supplier disputes the charge or just refuses to pay, then its bank should cough up anyway. But it may try to wriggle out of it and say your claim is invalid. It must then raise a dispute with the network – Visa, Mastercard or Amex. That payment network then examines the case and you may be asked for evidence or a statement. The network then makes a ruling, which is final. The banks involved have to abide by that – it is part of their contract with the network.

With a chargeback claim, your bank may refund the money quickly but warn you it may take it back again if the claim is disputed and you lose. That can be very annoying. If it happens it may be worth threatening to go to the financial ombudsman and see if your own bank will pay up.

Chargeback claims normally have to be made within 120 days of the payment. But if it is for a future event such as a concert and it is several months before you know something has gone wrong, then that can extend to 540 days. Always best to claim as soon as you know something is wrong. Chargeback does not apply to charge cards like Diner's Club.

Section 75 and chargeback cover goods or services that are defective, do not arrive, are cancelled, are fraudulent or where the firm goes bust. They do not apply if you just change your mind. If you bought it face to face or you are past the 14-day return time for something you bought remotely, then it is up to the retailer what they do. Some may give you a credit note. Some may do nothing.

Returns

Let me be clear about your absolute right to send something back. Originally an EU law, the right to return goods bought online or over the phone is becoming part of our shopping habits. Especially when we have been locked down or reluctant to shop face to face. You do not need a reason or an excuse. If something you ordered is delivered and you change your mind, you can return it without a reason if you inform the firm within 14 days and then return the item within another 14 days. Some people now treat this right as a normal part of shopping. Not sure which size will fit? Order a 10, a 12 and a 14 and send the two smaller ones back. Many online suppliers now provide pre-paid return labels and an easy process. But whether they do or not your online rights are absolute – return an item within the time limits and get your money back. You may have to pay postage, though that is often covered and if the website does not say you will have to pay return postage, then you can demand that back too. I call this an 'absolute' right, which it normally is, but it may not cover perishable or bespoke items (always try) and software may be exempt. However, it has emerged recently that online books are not exempt. So, it is possible to buy one, read it, and then return it electronically so it disappears from your library. However, I do not recommend this – especially if it is this book! It really is very unfair to authors who then get nothing as there has been no sale. I know you can borrow books from libraries and read them for free, but authors do get some money from that through Public Lending Right – about 8.5p a borrow. It is just not fair!

Foreign purchases

If you buy something from a foreign supplier that has no UK presence then your consumer rights may be harder to enforce. You can get help from the UK International

Consumer Centre, which is run by the Trading Standards Institute and gives free advice and assistance when you have problems with items or services bought from abroad: go to **ukecc.net**, email eccnet-uk@ec.europa.eu or call 01268 88 66 90. It is always better to buy through a UK retailer if you can as this keeps your rights simple and easier to enforce.

> *Money Box listener Geraldine messaged me after she had problems with a health device she bought direct from an American firm. It went wrong within a few weeks but when she complained – eventually to the CEO – she was told she had passed the 45-day return period it specified. I pointed her to UKICC:*
>
> *'Thanks Paul. You are a star.'*
>
> *Geraldine, via Twitter*

Remember

- Buy online and you can send things back for no reason within the time limits.
- Buy things for over £100 with a credit card and if things go wrong, you can get the money back from your credit-card provider.
- Buy with a debit card and if things go wrong, you should be able to get your money back from your bank.

HOW TO COMPLAIN

There is a word I won't use but as you know it happens. And when it does hit the fan, learning how, when and where to complain is a vital life skill. Read on!

THE FINANCIAL OMBUDSMAN SERVICE

The Financial Ombudsman Service is your friend – though a rather slow one at times. If you have a complaint about any regulated financial firm, whether it is a bank, a financial adviser, an investment firm, a platform or a claims management company, the FOS is the place to go. First, though, you must complain to the firm. Be clear and concise and state what you want. Say that if it rejects your complaint, you will go to the Financial Ombudsman Service. That shows you know what you're doing and the firm knows it will normally cost it £750, so it concentrates its mind. It has up to eight weeks to give you its decision. If that is 'no' or if it just does not respond for eight weeks, you go to the Financial Ombudsman Service (**financial-ombudsman.org.uk**), which has a useful 'how to complain' page that is worth reading before you start your complaint. The FOS upholds around four out of ten consumer complaints – more in some areas – and even if it says 'no' that is not the end of it. That initial decision is made by an adjudicator. But you – or the other side – can insist the decision goes to an actual ombudsman, like an appeal. The ombudsman's decision is binding on the firm – it must do what the ombudsman says. You can still pursue it through the courts if you want to.

It is free for you to go to the ombudsman. If the FOS says the firm must pay compensation for financial loss – that can be up to £355,000 – but if the firm cannot pay or goes bust rather than do so, then you can get your money from the Financial Services Compensation Scheme (FSCS) – **fscs.org.uk**. However, that may have a much smaller limit.

Remember that if an adviser recommends an investment and it does not do well, you cannot complain about that unless the adviser promised something that is not true. If you were mis-sold a product, you can complain, or if the adviser recommended a product that turned out to be fraudulent. You can also complain about insurance that does not pay up and banks that treat you unfairly or refuse to compensate you for a theft.

You can only get compensation for a regulated firm. Always check on the FCA register **fca.org.uk** and search 'register'. But do that before you use them, not after things have gone horribly wrong!

OTHER OMBUDSMEN

There are now ombudsmen, or what are called 'alternative dispute resolution' (ADR) services, for almost all businesses that sell to the public. Some are better than others. For ombudsmen covering telecoms and energy providers, go to **ombudsman-services.org**. If you have bought something and want to complain, try the Retail ADR – **retailadr.org.uk**. For flights, the Civil Aviation Authority is where you must go – **caa.co.uk** – though for many of those I prefer my nuclear option (see below) and that can be adapted for other complaints too.

If you want to complain to an individual firm, a useful tip is to find the email or phone number for the chief executive at a brilliant website **ceoemail.com**. That will make sure your complaint is fast-tracked. Complaining on Twitter to the firm's Twitter handle can also be good. They will often suggest taking it to private direct messages. Resist that, except for confidential details of course. The more public the complaint stays, the better.

THE NUCLEAR OPTION

During the Covid-19 pandemic, hundreds of thousands of people lost flights, holidays, events and bookings. In every case, they were entitled to a full refund. This is just a matter of law. If you pay for something and it is not provided, the firm has to refund you. Of course, these firms were terrified of the sheer scale of the money they had to find. So they tried to fob people off with vouchers. The other technique was to say well, yes, you can have a refund, but it will take us eight months to provide it. They did not put enough staff on their helplines and complaints by email were not answered. In other words, they created procedures to avoid doing what the law clearly and absolutely requires – a full refund.

The last thing you should do is to get stuck in the treacle field they spread. So I started promoting the nuclear option. I call it that because you threaten to use a weapon so powerful it terrifies everyone so much they will always want to avoid its use. I refer of course to the courts.

Although developed during Covid, the technique with minor amendments can be used in any case where the law gives you rights to your money back and the firm either refuses or simply does not reply to you.

- **Step 1:** Try the normal procedures. If customer service departments are functioning properly the nuclear option should not be needed. But if you try that and you are obstructed or ignored or lied to, then open the silo.

- **Step 2:** Start the process of taking your case to what we used to call the small claims court. You can do it online. In England and Wales, it is at **moneyclaim.gov.uk**. In Scotland, it is called the simple procedure at **scotscourts.gov.uk**. In Northern Ireland, go to **justice-ni.gov.uk** and search 'small claims'. These are for small claims up to a few thousand pounds but will cover the costs of almost all these consumer products we are talking about.

- **Step 3:** Fill in the claim form with your details and the firm's, the amount claimed and the reasons. This will cost you nothing. Just before you are asked for money, do not proceed further and take a screenshot of the page.

- **Step 4:** Ignore all the normal procedures that they set up with the specific purpose of fobbing you off. Every firm has a special fast-track for complaints that is used, for example, if a Member of Parliament complains or the chief executive's friend's cousin has a problem. Go straight to the boss. Again, use the marvellous website called **ceoemail.com**. Look up any firm or organisation and it will list the direct phone line and the email of the chief exec or managing director. Email them. Always be polite and to the point. Stress your rights and, if you can, quote the law you are relying on. Say you want your money back within seven days. That alone would get you to the fast-track. But then load the weapon. Attach the screenshot. That shows them you are not bluffing. You are not just threatening to take them to court – the missile is loaded and the button ready to be pressed.

In some cases it will not work. In which case, press that button and go to court. No firm will want the hassle of that. They will almost certainly settle before the hearing.

Boring bits

If the firm is foreign-owned – and some of the more notorious non-payers among the airlines are – then you may have to use the courts in the country where they are based. Check first at Companies House – free at **gov.uk** – search 'companies house' – to check if the firm has a UK subsidiary and sue that. If not, then google small claims court [country], for example, it might be Ireland. Most EU countries have a simple small claims procedure.

I have written about this nuclear option several times and done a blog on it. Feedback from delighted readers shows it works. It cuts the Gordian knot and releases your money.

> *'After a couple of frustrating weeks trying to contact EasyJet Customer Services, and with numerous emails to them and also to their CEO Johan Lundgren, all with no reply, I took your advice and set up a claim at moneyclaim.gov.uk. Within 24 hours of sending them the screenshot, I had a reply from someone in Executive Support prioritising our case and they are now refunding our full fares, in total £1611! Thanks for the advice and very much appreciated!'*
>
> *Bob, via email*

TRADING STANDARDS

If you think a business has broken the law or acted unfairly, you can report it to Trading Standards, which operates throughout England, Scotland and Wales. Complaints to Trading Standards are made via Citizens Advice **citizensadvice.org.uk** – search 'trading standards'. Find out more at **gov.uk** – search 'trading standards'. For complaints about foreign firms, see page 171 in Chapter 6.

COMPLAINING COW

The best book in the world about complaining is *How to Complain* by Helen Dewdney, who trades under the name Complaining Cow. She explains what the law is, how to write a complaint and who to. If you only buy one book about money apart from this one, make it hers.

GETTING SENSIBLE 41–60

CHAPTER 7

I am not quite sure when I got sensible but it was around this age! This chapter has all the things in it that count as 'being sensible' and – trust me – it is not as boring as it sounds. Because this is the age when you read things and think 'Oh, that seems sensible.' Finding pensions, putting spare cash (yes really!) somewhere good. Opening the Bank of Mum and Dad – as a lender not a borrower! – and making a will. Hmmm. That sounds sensible. I'll read that!

FIND THAT PENSION

You may already have several pensions that you don't even know about. That often happens when you move jobs. Look back on the jobs you have had. Do you know if there was a pension with them? I thought not! If you worked for a firm for more than two years, the chances are that pension is still there – a little – or maybe big – pot with your name on it.

There is an estimated £20 billion languishing in old pension funds that the owners have forgotten about. One of them could be you!

The government's Pension Tracing Service will help you find any pension schemes that you may have paid into. If you think you may have paid into a scheme through an old employer, the service will track it down from the name of your employer or the pension scheme. If you are not sure of those details and have no paperwork, then check with past workmates or use the free Companies House website. Go to **gov.uk** and search 'companies house'. Do NOT search on Google. You will get commercial services that want to charge you for free information.

It is not just workplace pensions that get lost. From the late 1980s there was a big drive to get everyone to take out a personal pension. But after four years, most people had stopped paying in. These lost pensions can be recovered too. If you have the old paperwork or at least the name of the provider or the scheme, the Tracing Service should be able to track it down.

The latest (though not very recent) figures show two out of three people who contacted the tracing service got up to £3000 lump-sum and nearly three out of four got a pension of up to £29 a week.

Beware firms that call themselves 'pension tracing service' but will either charge you or try to sell you advice or other services. Only search for it from gov.uk – do not use Google.

More information: **www.gov.uk** – search 'pension tracing service' or call 0345 6002 537.

CASH SAVINGS

Having confessed in the Investing section that I am not currently an investor, I also confess I like cash. And before you scoff, cash is still very popular, despite the very low interest rates that have been paid recently. Latest figures from the Bank of England (December 2021) show that there is £1.67 trillion – yes trillion, so that is £1,672,793,000,000 – in UK bank accounts, which is around £30,000 for every adult. And £259 billion is EARNING NO INTEREST! That does not just mean the nanorate of 0.01%, which Barclays paid until recently on its Everyday Saver account (Barclays UK profits in 2021: £8.4 billion), it means zero, zilch, nothing at all. In other words, money just sitting in current accounts. We are awash with cash.

It is hard to promote cash savings at a time of very low interest rates, which, until recently, ranged from the infinitesimal 0.01% – which would give £1 interest each year on £10,000 saved! – to the just visible under a microscope 0.25%. But in late 2022 things began to change. As I write, if you want access to your money immediately you can get 2.8%. But if you tie it up for a year, you might squeeze more than 4.5% out of it and more than that over five years. However, at the end of the five years, that may seem a very poor deal indeed as interest rates are currently rising and will probably continue to do so.

Saving in cash has the advantage that your money is completely safe. Put in £1000 today and you will still have £1000 and a bit more in a year or five years. If the very worst comes to the very, very worst and the bank you have your money in goes bust, then your savings are safe up to £85,000 – the Financial Services Compensation Scheme will repay you. So the ultracautious never put more than £85,000 into one bank or building society. The limit is per person, so in a joint account it is safe up to double that – £170,000. And if you have up to £1 million in an account following a house sale or a divorce or a major insurance payout, then it is safe up to that amount for six months.

Now at this point, investment professionals – who generally hate cash – will leap in and say that with inflation high and rising your money is worth less. So although it may still say £10 on the hundred tenners you take out, they will actually only buy stuff that you could buy for £500 today.

With inflation at 2% – which is the Bank of England target – money halves in value about every 34 years. And the average rate this century has been a little more than that at 2.2% or so. Which may not matter terribly. But with inflation at current rates – and I'm guessing it is more than 10% as you read this – money halves in six or seven years. And if we go back to the 1970s when inflation peaked at 25%, then money halves in value in just over two years. So inflation can eat away at your savings quite quickly.

Investment professionals hate cash for two reasons. First, their history is selling investments and earning commission. Before 2013, every time they sold an investment they were paid a percentage of the amount invested by the firm selling it. Then they got what was called trail commission every year after that – a small amount paid every year that the investment was held. If you put your money in cash savings, including National Savings & Investments, they got nothing. Second, in the long-term – see page 195 on Investing – investments have done better than the return on cash. So professional advisers feel safe recommending them and now, of course, they charge you a percentage of your assets held with them.

There is a big warning to be made regarding the statement 'investments outperform cash'. When the comparison is made – and the best known and relied on is called the Barclays Equity Gilt Study – the figures exaggerate the gap between investments and cash in two ways:

- The investment returns are too high because the figures take no account of the cost of investing – no deduction is made each year for the percentage deductions and other costs, they are simply based on how the various share indexes perform.
- The return on cash is not maximised. It uses the return on just one building society account, which, since 1998, has been Nationwide's Invest Direct account. In 2021, when the research for the 2022 Study was done, that account paid 0.01% and yet by the middle of the year the best no notice account on the market paid 0.5% – fifty times as much. Even Nationwide offered an account paying 0.4%. This gerrymandering exaggerates the gap between savings and investments hugely.

A fairer measure of cash performance is what I have called and trade-marked Active Cash™. Each year you put your money into the best one-year bond – in other words, the cash is tied up for a year. At the end of every year, you move your money to the best one-year bond, which will always be different. So, each year, for a year, you have a guaranteed rate. Using that and comparing the returns to a real tracker fund that matches the rise and fall of the FTSE100 index is a fairer comparison of cash vs shares.

In 2016, I did some research into how often a shares investment beat cash over the period from 1995 to 2016. It found that over five- and ten-year periods, cash was better than shares more often than not. And in some periods shares actually lost money, which of course cash did not.

My research was heavily criticised by the investment community, largely because of my choice of fund – the FTSE 100 tracker was just a daft thing to compare it to, I was told, though a quick look at other indices indicated similar results. I have not updated the figures over the last six years and no-one should take this research to be a recommendation not to invest, which, in the long-term, always beats cash.

But if you want to keep your money in cash, there is no doubt that Active Cash™ is the way to do it. The best-buy one-year bond is currently paying 4.5% – not huge but there is no risk. Shares can go down as well as plummet. Cash can only go up, slowly, often much slower than inflation, but it always goes up.

You can find the best-buys every day at **savingschampion.co.uk**. It also has a helpline operated by real people who know a lot. And if you have a lot of cash it will look after it for you, for a fee, recommending moves and helping you to make them.

Since I did my research, at least one other firm has tried to cash in on cash under the very similar name Active Savings. It will take on the job of moving your money between savings accounts without your intervention, though it will not always find the best as it only uses accounts with banks it has deals with.

BANK OF MUM AND DAD

I don't normally tell bank managers what to do – though I might tell them where to go! – but you are in charge of this bank now and it is up to you to make your own decisions.

House deposits

I told young people who wanted a deposit or a bigger one to buy their first home property that they should ring mum (Chapter 6 – see page 143). The bigger the deposit, the lower the debt and the lower the interest rate. Win-win. And it is one of the most popular things for the BOMAD to do. In a list of mortgage lenders, BOMAD would be in the top ten – maybe the top five. But now it is time for the caveats. That is Latin for 'take care or beware'. You see, it is fine if it is your son or daughter and they are buying their own first home. But what if it is one of them and their significant other who are buying? Relationships end. And if they are or get married, then your gift is half their other half's. If they are not married but joint owners, then ditto. And while your child may love that person and you may think they're OK (but of course they could have done better), everything could go pomaceous.

There is no easy answer to this conundrum – which is why it is a conundrum. I recommend the following:

- Do not take a stake in the property – most mortgage lenders would not be happy with that either.
- You could try to get your gift carved out in a pre-nup.
- Or perhaps better have it reflected in the share of the ownership of the property, so your daughter owned 55 per cent or 60 per cent (depending how big your gift was), while Mr O Half owned the rest. Again, check with the lender.
- Most important, be aware of it. And have the conversation beginning, 'Darling, you know I like Pete and you do seem very happy but …' In the long run they will thank you (well, Pete might not!).

Student loans

The other big dilemma for the Bank of Mum and Dad is should we pay off their student loan? In the past, for people going to uni between 2012 and 2022, the answer was no. No. That is because 80 per cent of those students never do pay off those student loans, so it is daft for you to do it in advance. Eight times out of ten you are just giving the government more money. But for the Class of '23 and beyond, the answer is not so clear cut. The interest rate has been reduced for higher earners and the time before it is written off extended from 30 to 40 years. About half of these students are expected to pay off their loans. So instead of a firm 'no', the answer is now an equally definite 'hmmm, maybe'. If you expect your child to do well and you want to save them the 9 per cent graduate tax on all earnings over £25,000, then the answer is probably 'yes'. But it is a fine balance. Except, of course, if they are blessed by being a Scottish student, in which case it is always 'yes'. If you can afford it, go ahead, but it won't cost them that much anyway. More details of the new loans on page 42 in Chapter 3.

MAKE A WILL

You may only be in your forties, but you are not immortal. Sorry to break it to you, but there will come a moment – whoops, someone in their forties has just discovered that too late. Every half hour or so in the UK someone in their forties dies, and the chances are they suffered from intestacy. No, that's not the cause of death! It means they did not have a will. Are you intestate? It is very silly.

If you don't leave a will

Who will get your stuff? Your home? Your money? That Chinese vase great-uncle Malcolm bought in Hong Kong and which everyone says is worth a fortune? The answer is it could be the Prince of Wales! If you have no living relative, everything goes to what is vaguely called 'the Crown' and, depending where you live, that can mean the Prince of Wales or the monarch. The details are slightly different in Northern Ireland and a bit more different in Scotland but wherever you live, the Crown gets your stuff if you don't make a will and have no living relatives. In some ways that might be better than it going to some distant relative who is alive of course! Because the lucky heir can be very distant. For example, if you have no spouse (or civil partner), no children or parents alive, then it starts spreading sideways to siblings (none of those either?), uncles, aunts, half-blood dittos and their children. All your stuff could go to your dead half-aunt's adopted grandson, who you have never met and quite frankly wouldn't want to.

Some people think making a will is morbid. But, in fact, it is a loving act. Without a will, your loved ones may face a struggle to sort out your estate and, perhaps more importantly, the people you want to get your money may not do so.

If you live with someone but are not married to them, then they have no rights at all. There is no such thing as a 'common-law' wife or husband, however long you have been together or had children and decorated the spare bedroom. If you die, they will not inherit your home, money or possessions and may be left homeless and destitute. The only way to be sure they get what you want is to make a will. Even in Scotland where the law is different – and, as usual, more sensible – the rights of bereaved live-in lovers are very restricted and they have to apply to the court for a share within six months of the death. They may not get it.

Even if you are married or in a civil partnership then your spouse (I use the term to cover both same and different-sex couples because the law applies identically to all of them) will not always inherit everything if you do not leave a will. If there are children, the surviving spouse gets the first £270,000 and then half of the rest. The balance goes to your descendants. In Scotland, the survivor gets more but not everything. If you have joint property and children from previous marriages, then things get very complex indeed. And if you do get married (or civil partnered) you should make a new will because in England, Wales and Northern Ireland that invalidates the one you made earlier. It doesn't do that in Scotland, but it is always better to make a new one in the light of a new relationship. And I don't mean to be unromantic – I'm not, honestly – but a pre-nuptial agreement is not a bad idea either, especially if you are partnering up late in life and each of you has different amounts of wealth. More on pre- and post-nups on page 92 in Love and Money.

How to make a will

Hire a solicitor

This is the safest way to make a will (and the only way to make a prenup). It will cost you a couple of hundred pounds or so – more with some solicitors and double that for a pair of wills for a couple – but you will be protected by a complaints procedure and the legal ombudsman. Sometimes solicitors will not charge. There are usually free wills months in March – 'Make a Will Week' – and in November – called 'Will Aid'.

Sort out your finances

What you own and what you owe – and who you want to get what. Keep your will as simple as possible. And you are not in the movies, so don't use it to settle old scores or make bad jokes. Keep it fair and reasonable. Remember, once you have died and your heirs have got probate, it will be published and anyone can get a copy online for £1.50 – unless you are in the Royal Family, which I am guessing you are not. It is more expensive and complicated in Scotland, but still possible and not that difficult.

Decide who will sort your affairs once you have gone

These people are called the executors. It is much better to trust this to a member of the family – preferably an heir – who can cope with a bit of admin. I would never name a solicitor or a bank to be an executor as they will charge a percentage of the value of your estate and may not be very communicative or helpful to your heirs. You cannot pay an amateur for being an executor but you could leave them some money in your will instead.

So. MAKE A WILL. And make sure that it is done properly and yes I do think that means using a regulated solicitor. Sorry will writers, I know you are cheaper than solicitors, but you are generally not legally qualified and you do not have the same protection if things go wrong. Similarly, do not use the stationery counter at W H Smith or that online wills place that comes top in a Google search. A solicitor will cost a bit more but it should be legal. And here's the kicker. if it is not done right, your relatives can sue someone and make another solicitor rich!

Solicitors tell me they make more money out of sorting out disputes over a badly drawn will than they do in making legally proper ones.

But your will is just half the job. While you've got all the details of your finances in front of you write a Letter of Wishes and also what an accountant I know calls a Dying Tidily letter.

Letter of wishes

A letter of wishes is like an annex to your will but – and it is a big BUT – it has no legal status. It simply expresses what you would prefer to happen and can be ignored by your executors or heirs. But it is still a good idea to say what you want to happen.

Some of your stuff will almost certainly end up in a charity shop so say which one you like. Maybe you should encourage fairness when it comes to your personal stuff – who gets what etc.. Perhaps a piece of jewellery or a valuable that you did not mention in your will should go to that favourite relative – no, not that one, THAT one. You should also say what should happen to your social media accounts – but safest if you have already dealt with that with the accounts themselves.

Finally, say how and where you want your remains to be left – buried, given to science or cremated. And if the latter, scattered or interred? Where? Orbit! Who do you think you are, Gene Roddenberry? You might want to say more about your funeral and wake. Or just tell people to do what will make it best for them. Because, as I often say, funerals are for the living not the dead. You won't know anything about it. Even when people smile bravely and say, 'She would have loved that bit!' and weep.

Remember, everything in a letter of wishes can be ignored. So, make sure the really important stuff is in your will.

Dying tidily letter

The third document is to help your executors. A dying tidily letter starts with where your will is (make an appointment with a solicitor to write one now if you haven't) and your letter of wishes. Tell the executors and your loved ones where the original is. And keep a copy with your death documents. Yes, you really should have a file called that.

The letter starts with you:

- **All your names.** (Not everyone knows the whole wonder of all of them.) Date of birth (not everyone knows that either, and will some of them be surprised!), address, previous addresses (really handy for some things) and National Insurance number.
- **All your money.** Bank and building society current accounts, savings accounts, National Savings & Investments, premium bonds, cash. If you have joint accounts, the other person can usually access those without ceremony after your death. Then investments if you have any and the firm that looks after them. For each item, say where the paperwork and computer files are. Also, any shop loyalty cards or air miles – there may be valuable points on them.
- **Your income.** Where does your income come from? Earnings, self-employment, pensions – including the state pension – other benefits, dividends, interest, annuities, rent and anything else.
- **Creditors.** If someone or some firm owes you money, list the full details here. The executors have a duty to recover it.
- **Fess up to your debts.** Where they are and what the repayments or deadlines are, be they mortgages, loans, catalogues, credit cards or pawn tickets.
- **Any property you own or own jointly.** Include any mortgage or equity release on it, any rent you earn with details and any agent you use. If you rent your home, your executors need to know where the tenancy

agreement and other documents are. Name of the landlord, the agent, your rent, the deposit you paid and which agency holds it. Your executor can recover this – once they have argued about the cost of cleaning the carpet from that time when you – oh, never mind. All forgotten now (except by the landlord).

- **Note your vehicles.** Car, van, caravan, boat, bike – where they are and any finance deals on them.
- **List your valuable items.** Write down what and where they are. Now is the time to say what to do with all that weird stuff you have collected over the years.
- **Storage.** Any storage unit or a safe or a bank safety deposit box you have. Write down the details including the access codes or where the keys are. Do not leave your will in one – your heirs will not be able to access the box until probate is granted. And probate can't be granted until … you guessed it!

A Money Box *listener wrote to me many years ago to say she was sure that her father had a Swiss bank account. He had mentioned it several times while tapping the side of his nose and promising it would see her all right. Of course, he never wrote down the ten-digit number that was the only way to access it. And when his heart stopped unexpectedly, the record he kept in his brain disappeared.*

- **Passwords.** Nowadays, it is more likely to be the 35-character access code to that bitcoin your dad bought in 2010, which at one time was worth £50,000 and even now is worth more than nothing – if you can find the key and access it and it wasn't a fraud in the first place! So write down your passwords. At least the one to your computer – and all those that might be needed to access social media, accounts and money. See page

277 in Chapter 10 for why it is safe to do this. And about the wormhole.

- **Insurances.** Life insurance that will pay out on your death, a funeral plan if you have one. (You shouldn't of course – see page 264 in Chapter 9. But if you did, your relatives might as well at least claim on it if they can.) List any other insurance that can now be cancelled.
- **Any pension you are paying into.** Where is it? Any old pension funds or entitlements you might have with a previous employer so your executors can track them down (see pension tracing on page 179).
- **Secret stuff.** Now's the time to write it down. Because now is the time not to care if anyone finds out.
- **Details of your tax affairs.** Especially if you have been in business or self-employed, they may be a little complicated. Or indeed other affairs. Charles Dickens and Wilkie Collins both revealed their secret loves in their wills. If you have given away money, property, shares or valuables in the last seven years, list those gifts with dates. If you have made regular gifts out of income, write that down as well. These things will help your executors know what needs to be included – or can be excluded – when they do an inheritance tax calculation. See inheritance tax on page 234 in Chapter 8.
- **Finally, do you have a financial adviser?** Write down their details. They should be able to sort out the things they dealt with. But hang on. You didn't? Well, in that case, you must explain where your pension fund is, where your investments are and, of course, where any cash is.

Print off the letter of wishes and the dying tidily letter and keep them with your Death Documents – in fact, together with your will, they ARE your Death Documents! Perhaps in a sealed envelope labelled in big letters 'not to be opened until after my death'.

No-one wants to die. But at least we can do it tidily.

INVESTING

You might need this chapter at any time in your life. So it has its own space. Do a dog ear so you can come back to it from anywhere else in the book. It does what it says in the title.

Let's get one thing clear. Saving and Investing are two completely different things. With saving, you put money in an account with your name on it. It stays yours. And when you want it or need it, you go on your app and move it to your spending account. The money is yours. Always.

Investing is an entirely different thing. You lend your money to someone else. They then use it to buy shares or bonds or investments that you probably do not understand. That means they lend it to someone else. The hope is that the clever people third or fourth in the chain will make enough profit from that money to cover their costs and a bit more for profit, and then your share of the money will grow. And when you need it, it will be sold and, after charges, there will be more than you put in. Money making money. Or, as it is often called, putting your money to work. But all the time that money is lent out, it is not yours. All you have is a bit of paper saying they will pay you back. Usually.

Then there are three golden rules of investing:

- **Rule 1:** Do not invest if you have debt. Pay off the debt instead. That is because you can never earn more with an investment or savings than you will pay on a debt. Suppose you are given £1000 from a kind aunt or a bonus at work. If you have a credit card and generally it has a debt of around £1000 on it, then it will probably cost you at least £250 a year just in interest. Use the £1000 to pay it off and you will be £250 better off each year. But if you invest that £1000 or put it in a savings account, you will get 3% or 4% net return, which is £30 or £40. So paying off debt gives you a better return than saving or investing. Only invest or save when the debts have gone.

Like any rule – even golden ones – there are exceptions. A mortgage is different from normal debt so you might well want to save or invest if your only debt is your mortgage. Having said that, paying down your mortgage is a very practical way of reducing your monthly payments and ending up mortgage-free much sooner – which is a great feeling. The other exception is that some debts cannot be paid off without paying a penalty. So you must work out if it is worth paying it off and paying the penalty or just letting it run on for its allotted span.

- **Rule 2:** Put some cash aside. Investments must be long-term. But life is often short-term – you lose your job, fall ill, have a baby, fall out of love or whatever. So you need some cash to make sure you can pay your bills during a gap in your earnings. Three months' pay is a good target. Just sitting there in cash waiting for that rainy day. And earning a bit of interest of course.

- **Rule 3:** Investment is for the long-term. So bitcoin is not an investment, it is a gamble. So is gold. So is money flipping (see page 46 in Social Media). These are all gambles. Only invest if you can do it for the long-term. And more on what that means later!

SHARES

When people think of investing they often think of buying shares. A share is, believe it or not, a share of a company. It is usually a very small share – perhaps less than a billionth. But if you own one share, you own that one billionth of the company. Vodafone, for example, has 26.8 billion shares. So if you buy 27 shares, you own about one billionth of the firm. At the time of writing, each share was worth about 133.6p, making the whole company worth £1.336 x 26.77 billion = £35.85 billion – in round terms. If you own shares, you can make money in two ways.

Dividends

Each year the company will pay some of the profit it makes to shareholders (that's you). That is called a dividend on each share you own. Some years it will pay more than others. They won't distribute all the profits – they will keep some of them for investments or a working balance or to set aside for legal battles and, of course, they have to pay the chief executive and other directors more money each year than you will probably ever see in your lifetime. Vodafone certainly does.

Buying a fund

The value of your shares will go up and down but, overall, you hope the value will rise. For example, in Vodafone's case the shares now are almost as low as they have ever been. If you had bought them at the start of this century, they were 730p each. Now they are less than a fifth of that. But as recently as October 2020, they were 103p, so if you had bought them then you would have made a good gain over recent years. Predicting which firms will do well and when and which badly is at the heart of investing. Unfortunately, almost everybody is very, very bad at it. So, it is best not to do it. If you want to see how one knowledgeable journalist bets his own money, try Ian Cowie's 'Personal Account' in the Business and Money section of *The Sunday Times*.

Instead of doing it themselves, people generally buy what is called a fund. There are two sorts of fund (actually there are loads of different sorts, but this will get us going). They are called active and passive. At least that is how they are described. But in the Lewis Carroll world of investment jargon, what things are called and their name are two, or even half a dozen, entirely different things:

- **An actively managed fund** has someone in charge of it who tries to get right those guesses about what will go up and what will come down. They use their skill and insight to buy or sell at the right time. They can make money on shares they expect to fall in value as well as those they expect to rise. By doing that, they hope to keep your money growing. The problem is, no fund has ever grown more than the whole market over the long-term. So although these people are very, very well paid (they might earn more than the Vodafone boss earns in his life), you can never be sure their funds are the best place for your money.

  In January 2022, Jupiter Fund Management was forced to justify a £60.5 million performance fee paid to just two of its fund managers – around one pound in every twelve of the value of the fund.

- **The other sort of fund is passive.** They are usually called trackers because they buy shares in every company in a particular index – such as the FTSE 100, which you will no doubt hear quoted on the news every day. And then they just sit tight and see where the index goes – they 'track' the index. Any dividends paid are

> reinvested so your money benefits from the compound interest effect on those. In the long-term, all the research shows that passive trackers are likely to make you more money than active funds.
>
> There are hundreds, thousands, of trackers and they track different indices and charge you different amounts for doing so. Because they have to hold all the shares in an index, when the companies in the index change they have to sell shares in the departing companies at just the wrong time – because everyone else is selling them – and buy the shares in the newly promoted companies when everyone else is buying them – yep, at exactly the wrong time too. Those charges are paid for out of your money. So they are not perfect.

When you buy a share of a fund you can think of it as a little pot with your name on it and say 1000 units of that fund inside it. There is a lid on the top to which you have the key. So you can decide when to add more units or when to take them out. But that key is a deception. There is also a side door so the fund manager can reach in and swap your shares for others using their skill or to match the tracker. Every time they buy or sell shares there is a cost – the buying price is always more than the selling price – it's called the turn and guess who pays it? You. There is a third way into – or rather out of – your pot. At the bottom there is a little tap. And once a month or year the fund will open it and take a percentage of your money. You will remember this from the section on pensions in Chapter 5. Charges range widely and although they are better than they used to be – by which I mean smaller and more transparent – they are still there and not always that clear. Worst of all, the charge that comes out is exactly the same regardless of whether the fund manager has done their job to make your money grow or not. Even if it halves in value, the same percentage of what's left will come out. Charges are the one thing you can control. So always pick the fund that charges the least. Charges are not related to the fund's performance as countless studies have shown. Just keep that tap on the bottom as tight as it can be. And limit the ins and outs through the side doors too by going passive.

Investment trusts

The same is true for investment trusts, which work in a similar way but there will be other things in them – property, for example, or corporate bonds. Historically investment trusts have provided a more consistent return than shares in companies. But that does not mean the investment trust you choose will do better. Indeed, read about Woodford on page 203 for one that did very badly.

Despite all this cynicism, in the long-term a good investment will do better than cash, probably. But long-term is long-term, not a few years – at least a decade and preferably two.

BONDS

What is a bond? Well, it can be anything from something 100 per cent safe to something 100 per cent dangerous. So don't trust the word 'bond' without research. A bond is a promise – as in 'my word is my bond' – and if you buy one the promise is you will be paid a fixed rate of interest for a fixed period and, at the end of that time your capital will be returned. But a bond is only as safe as the firm giving its word that the annual income will be paid and your money returned at the end. Nowadays, that promise can be a bit of paper, an email or just a number on a computer.

Premium bonds

These are 100 per cent safe and earn interest of 2.2% a year, which is put into a prize fund and paid out at random to 118 billion bonds held by 21 million people. Each month each bond has a one in 24,000 chance of winning a prize. The prizes are tax-free and almost all are for £25. They are a good deal if you pay higher rate tax and can afford to buy the maximum £50,000 bonds. You then have a good chance of winning two prizes every month. The actual rate of return – ignoring all the big prizes, which you won't ever win – is more like 2% tax free. What, never? Even if you held the maximum £50,000, you would have to wait over 99,000 years to have an even chance of winning the monthly £1 million prize. That long ago our species of humans were nomad hunter-gatherers with stone tools. A few had just begun to migrate northwards towards Europe. We had not even begun painting in caves. That is some wait. Even a £1000 prize would be won on average only once or twice in a lifetime – every 45 years – by someone with £50,000.

Bank or building society fixed-term bonds

These are normally called fixed-rate savings accounts. You get a fixed percentage return for a fixed period from one to five years. They are also 100 per cent safe – even if the bank or building society goes bust, your savings are protected up to £85,000.

Government bonds

Often called 'gilts', for 'gilt-edged', because they are completely safe. Buying and selling them is more difficult and you probably need advice. By trading in them you are gambling on the future of interest rates. That is best left to professionals. Currently new bonds are paying 0.5% over six years. But in the past they paid more, some linked to inflation.

Corporate bonds

These are issued by a company. You lend it £1000 and it promises to pay you, say, 3% a year for five years. You get £30 a year income and at the end of the five years, you get your £1000 back. But that depends on the company surviving. So they are risky. Companies use them as a way to raise money rather than borrowing it from a bank. Treat with caution.

All other bonds are risky and should be avoided. You can buy bonds in property investments or works of art or stamps or wine. It is just a way of wrapping a high-risk investment – or a scam – in the trustworthy word 'bond'.

WHEN TO START INVESTING

The best time to start investing is in your twenties. First, because if something goes horribly wrong you have a lot of life left to make up any losses. And secondly, if everything goes tolerably well, compound interest will do its job with interest earning interest on interest. But very few people do it then because that is the time when your money runs out before your month does. So, the best time to start investing is usually a decade or two ago.

But now your twenties are half a lifetime away and you are finally just about beginning to think, 'Hmmm, maybe I'm not immortal.' And, more to the point as no-one likes thinking about death, 'I don't want to be poor in retirement, so I want to put my money to work, not earning 2% in a savings account.'

Let me say right upfront – I don't do investment. I'm not expert in it nor am I qualified to give advice. I see it from the outside and a lot of it isn't very pretty. But if you want to make money in the long-term (and we will discuss how long long-term is later) then investment is the way to go. But you must be careful.

There are several reasons why I don't invest – which is a decision that has probably cost me a lot of money over the last thirty years – one of them is the same as why I don't gamble. The thrill of winning for me is so much weaker than the pain of losing that there is no fun in it at all. So, I have never bought a lottery ticket, which actually has saved me a lot of money. When I was in an office, I did not take part in the Grand National sweepstake, and I don't run across the road without looking because it is so much quicker, as long as you do actually get to the other side. Sorry. That is just me.

Even sure-fire investments can burn you badly. Neil Woodford was a man with the Midas touch. At one point he was looking after £12 billion of his clients' money. Over 25 years, he had turned £10,000 into £255,000. He – and those who hitched their wagon to him – couldn't lose. Until they did. In June 2019 his fund – which had been taking riskier and riskier bets – was put into administration. As I write, investors have lost around a quarter of their money. And although there may be a little more to come back, the best hope is a loss of about a fifth of it.

ETHICS

A lot of the finance industry seems to think ethics is a county east of London. And at one time, people did not care where their invested money went or what it was used for. The return was all that mattered. Ethical investing was as weird as not wearing leather or being vegan. Now, of course, it is mainstream. Ethical or green investing is big business. Of course, it isn't called that anymore. It is referred to as ESG. Why use plain simple words when an obscure TLA can be used instead? ESG is Environmental, Social, Governance. Still no clearer? Environmental is pretty straightforward – no money in oil production or mining for a start. Social? Well, that means firms that do good rather than bad. Nothing in tobacco where the products kill their customers slowly and often painfully. Including my father, so forgive me if I am particularly down on that industry. And please don't think that vaping is about doing good either. Doctors used to recommend smoking. And Governance? Well, this means running a business that is ethical. One that pays its staff well and treats them like humans. And when it sources goods or materials from distant parts of the planet, it makes sure they are not cheap because they have been made by children or slaves. They should also check that the manufacturing process of those items does not break E or S. For example, to keep profits up, the factory pumps out waste into the local river where people bathe and drink. Or wages are so low that instead of work lifting people who work there out of poverty, it traps them in it.

So, really ESG means green, green/ethical and ethical. But you will see ESG far more than you see those plain simple words. Like any new fad – and that is what it is – the industry sees it as little more than a marketing exercise. In 2021, out of £43.2 billion freshly invested by individuals, £16 billion was put into funds labelled ESG – that is more than a third. However, research by the consumer group *Which?* found that some of the biggest socially responsible funds included major oil companies and firms linked to deforestation. When challenged, the funds said that the firms were committed to go net-zero by 2050. So that's all right then! Always look behind the label or get a good independent financial adviser who you trust to do that for you. EIRIS has useful information about ESG at **eirisfoundation.org**. And in case you are still wondering, TLA stands for Three Letter Abbreviation!

One short cut to ethical is to go with Sharia investments or, indeed, savings. Sharia means that investments conform to the standards of Islam. Now, to be clear, I do not have a religious atom in my body, but Sharia products are what most would mean by ethical. Lending money at interest is banned – so you won't find a bank or doorstep lender in your Sharia investment. Alcohol is a no-no too, of course, as is gambling. Anything involving pork products or weapons is also excluded, as is pornography. There is a touch of realism added – and my Muslim readers will forgive me – that these things are not absolutely, completely and 100 per cent banned. But any firm that derives the majority of its income from them is. Sharia compliant funds have a board to oversee them and an annual Sharia audit to check. If it is found that there is interest charged somewhere, then it is taken out and donated to charity. Of course, that costs money, not least because – and forgive me again – Muslim scholars, like religious scholars everywhere, disagree and argue with each other about exactly what things mean and where the boundary of Sharia-compliant lies. But for Muslims, Christians and atheists alike, Sharia-compliance pretty much sits, as one investment guide puts it, 'within the ESG universe'. Honestly, why do they write like that? And it is worth remembering that not so long ago, Christians did not allow lending at interest either. And if you want to see scholars arguing over financial matters, please google that to check it!

If you want to be ethical, green or Sharia, of course it means you cannot do the simple thing in investing – buying a tracker that follows an index like the FTSE 100 or the New York S&P 500. Because in that index there will be firms that are so far outside the ESG universe that even the *Starship Enterprise* would not venture there. Never one to miss an opportunity, the finance industry has created ethical indexes. And if you talk to fans of ethical investing, you will find they claim that these indexes do as well or better than the more straightforward ones.

LONG-TERM

The thing about investments is they can go down as well as plummet. Of course, in the long-term you expect them to go up. And they do. Nearly always. But how long is long-term? A rule of thumb is twenty years, definitely. Ten years, probably. Five years, possibly. And by writing those numbers as words, I am indicating that these are not actual, definite precise amounts of time. They are the sort of durations you should be looking at. The first question your financial adviser – if you have one and see page 210 for how to find a good one – should ask is 'How long will you leave this money invested?' or 'What is this money for?' which will enable them to deduce that. But financial advisers like to use obscure jargon and may actually say, 'What is your time horizon?' or some such nonsense. In fact, if the one you try out does say 'time horizon' or, come to that, 'ESG universe', it may be worth making your polite goodbyes and moving down your shortlist of who to trust with your money.

FINANCIAL ADVICE

My first question now is, do you need financial advice? Unless you have a big lump-sum (tens of thousands of pounds) or a lot of surplus income to invest (hundreds of pounds a month), you probably don't need financial advice and probably will not want to pay the fees good advisers charge.

So, let us start with how to get good free financial advice. Or rather, where not to get it:

- **Do not get advice from social media.** TikTok, Twitter, Instagram, Facebook or any other social media service cannot ever give you good financial advice. OK, if you want to lose all your money in get-rich-quick scheme they are great. You can find one in a few moments. If you want some teenager explaining his marvellous new discovery called compound interest, which will turn £20 a week into a million pounds by the time you retire, guaranteed, then social media is your friend. But I think there are much easier and nicer ways to throw your money away. Like taking £1000 in tenners out of your bank, hiring a hot air balloon on your credit card and showering the villages below with banknotes. At least the people who get it won't be thieves. Never, ever, ever use social media to research investment. It's like fish researching the world above the water by sampling the food fishermen throw in. More on this on page 45 in Social Media.

- **Do not use Google or Bing to find things.** Top of your searches will come paid-for services that may or may not be suitable for you. One thing is for sure, they will be trying to make money out of you rather than for you.

Google is now supposed to ban ads from financial firms that are not regulated. Some financial services and investment do not have to be regulated. So sales of riverside apartments, wine *en primeur*, cask whisky, bitcoin, contemporary art, blockbuster films or NFTs (Non-Fungible Tokens) are all unregulated and unsupervised. Any crook can sell them and often does. A search on Google will find ads for these at or near the top of your search.

I repeat:

- **Rule 1:** Don't get financial advice from people on social media.

- **Rule 2:** Never respond to an advert on Google. They begin with Ad in bold before the url. But not everything dangerous that comes up is an ad. So just don't search.

DO NOT TOUCH – Buying off-plan

A rubbish investment offer arrives almost every day in my inbox. Let me warn you about one sort. Riverside apartments. They all offer similar things. A guaranteed rate of return, like '9% net assured returns for five years'. Glossy brochures will promise 'Close to amenities. Stunning views. Sought-after postcode. Waterside location.' And, of course, 'Easy payment plan'. Some of this is just the normal sell for new-build apartments. But these investment properties are often not built. They are just an artist's impression. It is called buying 'off-plan' and it is not unknown for the development never to be built. Even if it is, you have no idea 'off-plan' what the quality will be or how long they will last. You will probably not be told about the expenses, such as service charges, management costs or restrictive covenants, and, generally, you will have no idea at all of the demand or whether the rents needed to produce the returns can be secured. If they are already built, why are they being marketed so far away from the building itself? That is why they are in my DO NOT TOUCH box.

Free advice

Your first stop for free advice is the MoneyHelper website **moneyhelper.org.uk**. That is the new name for what used to be called the Money Advice Service and then was called the Money and Pension Service (MaPS). Its website is very good on a whole range of money issues, some of which many financial advisers will know little or nothing about.

If you have pension questions, then you can contact the Pensions Advisory Service, which has a helpful helpline on 0300 123 1047. That is also now part of MoneyHelper. It is free and – don't let this put you off – approved by the government.

Specific advice about the pension freedoms that began in April 2015 can be found at Pension Wise – see page 218 in Chapter 8 for pension freedom. If you are over 50, you can call 0300 330 1001 to book an appointment for one-to-one telephone advice, or a face-to-face interview at a nearby Citizens Advice office. Again, Pension Wise is now part of MoneyHelper.

INVESTING YOURSELF – PLATFORMS

Of course, not everyone has a financial adviser. There are many do-it-yourself investors and they usually nowadays use what is called a platform. There you catch the train to the magic money tree. Or not. A platform is just an online service that allows you to buy and sell funds or shares and keeps track of them and their value 24/7 – a bit like an online bank account. Except they are not free. A platform sits between an investor and their money and takes a little bit off it every time you buy or sell or even if you don't – just as time passes. For example, £25 a month just for sitting there and £8 for every sale or purchase. In addition, they will charge a small percentage of all the funds you hold with them. Perhaps a quarter of one per cent. But if your funds are worth £500,000, that is £1250 a year for, well, just sitting there. And if they have hundreds of thousands of customers – well, as the Americans say, do the math. Platform income can exceed half a billion pounds a year, for doing very little except keeping the tech running. No wonder it is the owners of platforms rather than their investors who are in the *Sunday Times* Rich List. But customers value the service and the ease of using these platforms and if you want to invest yourself, it is a good way to keep track of things. Just be aware that it is not free and the cost must be taken off any profit you make on your investments.

If you invest yourself you will not be given 'advice'. But you may well get newsletters and lists of funds that their experts think are good value. They may not be. In evidence of that I will just say ten words – Hargreaves Lansdown (a platform) Woodford Equity Income Fund (an investment). Google them together.

FIND A FINANCIAL ADVISER

The only people who can give you real proper financial advice about investments – including pensions – are regulated financial advisers who are registered with the Financial Conduct Authority. They must meet high standards but that does not mean they will always give you good advice. Nor does it mean that if they give you bad advice you can get your money back. But you should only ever use a regulated professional financial adviser. Remember that anyone can call themselves a 'financial adviser', an 'investment manager' or a 'property specialist'. And they do. All those terms are meaningless. All these people are allowed to operate unregulated as long as they only sell unregulated investments in things like whisky, property or art. Your money is completely at risk. In fact, it may be gone as quick as a bottle of Scotch mist.

If you want regulated financial advice, then I have a three-point plan to filter out the ones that you should not use. I have been accused of being very harsh with my filters. I take that as a compliment because I am.

Filter One: Independent

Only ever use an independent financial adviser or IFA.

Under the Financial Conduct Authority rules, there are two sorts of financial advisers. The sort you want are called 'independent'. That can mean one of two things:

- They give advice on all financial matters and look across the whole of the market and give that advice on any financial topic where they might recommend a product.
- They give advice on a specific type of product – such as annuities or pensions – and not on other types of products. But they must still look across the whole of the market relating to that product. This may be called 'focused independent' or may just be called 'independent'.

Any adviser who is not independent does not look at the whole of the market and may be tied to one or more firms and can only recommend products from those firms. These advisers are called 'restricted', though you will not find any of them using that term. Even though they try to keep it quiet you can sus them out by asking one simple question – do you offer independent financial advice? If the answer is anything but a clear 'yes', then reject them. Many restricted advisers work for a bank or insurance company or a large national network. They only recommend you buy their products. That is just sales masquerading as advice. Others may have what they call a panel of firms and will tell you they select them rigorously and it is cheaper for them to work that way. Just say 'bye'.

Some people call themselves International Financial Advisers, which they abbreviate to IFA, trying to give the impression that they are independent financial advisers. They are not and are probably not even regulated. Reject them out of hand. A firm that starts with a deceit often ends with a scam.

Filter One is harsh because there are some good financial advisers who are not independent. I tell them passing through Filter One is easy – stop being restricted.

That has sorted out the wheat from the chaff and now we want the very best ears of corn we can find.

Filter Two: Planners

Only ever use an IFA who is a chartered or certified financial planner.

The very best qualified financial advisers are chartered (or certified) financial planners. This brings you down to the best qualified 6000 or so of the 33,000 regulated independent financial advisers. They have put a lot of effort into being the good guys and the chances of a bad guy or gal remaining in there is small. As well as chartered individuals, a firm can be chartered, which means that at least some of their advisers are chartered themselves and the rest are probably working towards it. You can usually trust them too. Sadly, many good advisers will be rejected by Filter Two. Again, the answer is in their own hands. Get the qualifications.

Filter Three: Pay in pounds

Now we come to the most controversial of my three filters. Pick a financial planner who you can pay in pounds.

If you think that is an odd thing to say, you have not yet tried to find one. Many advisers – even the best that are left after Filters One and Two have done their work – will want to charge you a percentage of your money. Charging a percentage is like taxing your wealth. Drip, drip, every year some of your wealth becomes theirs. Even the taxman is not entitled to do that. Percentage fees are a hangover from the days of commission, when advisers lived on a percentage of the money their clients had invested paid by the product providers. This trail commission came in year after year, whatever they did or didn't do.

So, ask to pay in pounds. What do you charge for that report? How much is that service? If your eyes start to water when the sum is mentioned, then you probably do not need or cannot afford financial advice. A percentage seems small. It is not. It compounds up over the years. And it will pretty soon reach that eyewatering sum in pounds.

In some limited circumstances, a small percentage charge of around 0.5% of your money can be better value than paying in pounds. But always make sure that you check each year how much has been taken from you and review the service you get. Then you can see if it is value for money or not. If it's not, then find another adviser.

Once these filters have done their work, you will have gone a long way towards finding good, safe, but often expensive financial advice. Sadly, I have to point out that there are a small number of well-qualified independent financial advisers who have given dreadful advice, have gone out of business, or have even turned out to be crooks. So these three filters are not a guarantee but they are a good start.

Website research

You are probably wondering where you can find the advisers to apply your filters to. That raw material comes from online directories, of which there are several. Advisers may pay to be part of these directories and in the past could pay for higher positions. That should not happen now with the three below but be aware of it.

- I start with **AdviserBook**. No-one pays to be included and it has a complete list of more than 12,000 FCA-regulated firms of advisers. It states clearly which are verified as independent. You can also filter by qualifications and specialisms and how they charge you. So you can use my three filters on them to find the best. **adviserbook.co.uk**
- The oldest directory is called simply **Unbiased**. It was the first real attempt at a comprehensive database. It lists more than 18,000 independent financial advisers and does not allow restricted ones in at all. So that is Filter One passed! Although advisers can have a basic listing free, they can also pay a fee so that they can be contacted by a click through on the site. You will see a list of the 'top 20' near your postcode, which should be based on how near they are to you. You can use the site to apply my other filters and you even pick a male or a female adviser. **unbiased.co.uk**
- A newer database called **VouchedFor** uses algorithms to provide a list of advisers for you. They are ordered to take account of how local they are to you but also by using reviews and ratings by customers. Those push them up the list. Advisers cannot pay for a better position. The site checks all qualifications at the start and then periodically confirms them. Each entry shows clearly if the adviser is independent or restricted – always reject the latter of course. You can also filter by speciality and by qualifications. Each entry also shows the minimum amount of money you need for them to take you on as a client. So that is another useful filter if you have a bit less than £500,000! **VouchedFor** lists about 8000 financial advisers who choose to pay the fees to be included and of those 3000 are fully vouched for – you can only click through to the adviser website for those. **vouchedfor.co.uk**

Use these sites to draw up a shortlist. Then do one final test – their website. I would only use an IFA who has a website where you can find out more. Ignore the slick sales patter, which usually reads as though it is generated by a PR machine – it probably was as you will find similar meaningless platitudes on most of them. The key question is: does it tell you what they charge? I would tend to prefer those that do but, as with all my filters, that will exclude some people who may be OK. Some advisers have justified hiding their charges by saying it would only confuse customers! Others find that it is good business to make them clear and transparent. If you do pick one that keeps its fees secret, your first question when you meet them should be about charges and costs. If the answer is anything but clear, that is a warning flag. Also, ask what it will be in pounds (if they haven't told you) and then ask what you get for that fee.

Most advisers will give you one free session. Go prepared with details and information about yourself. Try two or three and see which you prefer. Do not be embarrassed to say 'no' to them.

Breaking up

If you pick an adviser but later regret your choice, you can leave by just writing a letter telling them they are no longer your adviser. Ask them to return any documents and destroy all your data. If you feel you have been badly advised or locked into investments you did not want, then complain and ask for compensation. If they still say no (or if they say nothing at all after eight weeks), pursue the complaint to the Financial Ombudsman Service. That will usually cost them £750 so it may speed things up to threaten that first before doing it – see page 173 in How to Complain.

Hugh had a problem with bad advice. Go to the Financial Ombudsman Service, I emailed. He replied:

> *'Your assiduous attention to your emails ... and the excellent advice of yourself and your team on* Money Box *are much appreciated.'*
>
> *Hugh, via email*

Finally, if you are ever cold called or receive a text or email from an adviser you have not found and researched, just say 'no'. In fact, just say nothing. Delete it or end the call. No-one ever lost money by doing that. Many have lost money by not doing that.

Remember

- Investing can seem complicated – it is – so think carefully and get help or advice before you start.
- Funds that track markets as they go up or down are cheaper and more likely to produce better returns in the long-term.
- Investing does not have to be unethical.
- Good financial advice comes at a price but is worthwhile if you have a lot to invest.
- There is some good free advice available but beware anyone who offers you that who is trying to make money out of you.
- If anyone cold calls about an investment, always say 'no'.
- Read the section on social media.

CHAPTER 8

PREPARING TO WIND DOWN 55–70

Tick tock. Winding down. I must say when I was 55, or even when I was 70, I did not like the idea of winding down. Of course, I was lucky. I can do my job as long as I can stagger to a keyboard or microphone. The work many people do requires physical strength, which does begin to decline after 50. And others hate their jobs so much that retiring for them is looking forward to a 30-year holiday. And, of course, people become unwell and their job just gets too demanding. But, let's face it, 50 is pretty certainly more than halfway there. So, tick tock. Time's wingèd chariot and all that. So this

chapter looks at all the things you should be aware of – and beware of – now that you are on the gentle slope down.

PENSION FREEDOM

Let's start with the positives. In your fifties and sixties you can still pay into a pension. Okay, the investment growth will not be that much between now and when you want to take it out. But you get tax relief. I can't stress that enough. Here are a few examples:

- You pay in £100 out of your taxed income and, hey presto, as if by magic £125 goes into your pension fund. And when you do take it out, a quarter, £31.25, is tax-free and the rest is taxed. So, you put in £100. After tax is paid, you take out £106.25. It is a money-making machine. If you pay higher rate tax, the arithmetic is even better.

- You can put in as much as you like up to £40,000 a year (including the tax subsidy), but it cannot be more than your earnings.

- If your earnings are below £3600 gross – even as low as zero – you can still put in up to £2880, which magically becomes £3600 in there. So if you can, put money into a pension.

Once you have tracked down your pensions (see page 179 in Chapter 7), you can think of taking them out.

Resist temptation

Fifty-five is a great age. No, seriously, it is. You can take your pension! Yes. At 55 with thirty or so years of life left, you can put your feet up and retire. Or at least you can take out your pension. **Here's a word of advice. Don't.**

There are very few people who have saved enough in a pension to be able to retire comfortably at 55. Or even 65. A sobering analysis of what you need to have saved for a 'comfortable' retirement at 65 was published last year. About a quarter of a million pounds for a 'comfortable' life and £800,000 for a luxurious one. By that they mean, for a couple between them – an income of £22,000 a year or £40,000. That is the guaranteed income for life that those huge sums will buy you.

Of course, the temptation is there. Since pension flexibility began in 2015, just over five million people have ignored my advice and taken out more than £42 billion. Which is around £8000 each. Most of them have not taken any advice at all about whether to do it. But it is something you are free to do. Mostly.

If you read page 117 in Chapter 5, you will remember there are two sorts of pensions. Quick recap:

- Schemes that promise to pay you a proportion of your salary when you reach pension age – say 1/80th of your salary for each year in the scheme. So after 40 years, you will get 40/80ths or half your annual pay until you die. For doing nothing. Oh, and some or all of that pension in theory will rise each year with inflation or close to it. However, many have a cap of 5% or 2.5% on that increase, which is way below the current rate of inflation. Nowadays, these salary-related pensions are called 'defined benefit', usually abbreviated to DB just to stop anyone really understanding what they are.
- Schemes that promise you nothing as far as your pension is concerned but just define what contributions you (and your boss if you have one) will pay. When you reach pension age, you take the pot of money that has accumulated over your working life (or more likely

over the years you have worked there) and try to buy something to eke it out over your retirement. These are called 'defined contribution' schemes or, of course, DC. All auto-enrolment pensions are DC. As are pensions you buy for yourself outside of work.

DB schemes are much better. But pension freedom is mainly about people with DC schemes. And because most people have more than one job in their lifetime – probably around six for people of your age – there may well be several pensions that you might be tempted to cash in.

Your DC pension

Pension freedom is simple for DC schemes. You just ask for your money. A quarter of it is free of tax (it can be more, make sure you check) and the rest is taxed.

If your income is £18,000 and you withdraw all your pension fund worth £20,000, then £5000 of that will be tax-free and the balance is added to your income and taxed, so you should pay basic rate tax of 20% on the balance of £15,000, which is £3000.

However, that is not how it works. The taxman routinely takes more than he should. Well, that is a bit unfair because strictly speaking he just follows the rules, which are daft, and then leaves you to sort it out.

HMRC assumes that the £15,000 you get from cashing in your pension fund will be a regular **monthly** income. If only!

HMRC converts that to an annual income – £15,000 x 12 (months) = £180,000 per year.

It then taxes you at a higher rate of tax to reflect that income. How much is deducted depends on the time in the tax year you take the money. If you did it in April, then instead of taking off the £3000 tax that is due, HMRC would deduct tax of more than £5000 from your lump sum – an extra £2000 in tax that you do not owe.

The calculations are complicated and these are just approximate examples. The exact amount deducted will depend on your tax code and when in the tax year you take the money out.

Getting your money back from the taxman

The important thing to remember is that the tax deducted from your pension lump-sum will almost certainly be too much and you must make sure you get this money refunded.

You can get it back in one of two ways:

- Wait until after the end of the tax year in April, by which time HMRC will realise your annual income is not what it has calculated and will give you a tax rebate.

OR

- Apply to get it refunded right away.

I would always get the money back as soon as you can. It is your money, not HMRC's, and it is better in your hands. Only when you get the tax deduction corrected will you know exactly how much of your pension pot will be left after tax.

Why is it taxed at all? Well, because when you paid money into the pension that was free of income tax. So, it is taxed on the way out. Or at least the three-quarters of it that is not tax-free.

Of course, to get back the tax you are owed involves filling in a form. It is always a form that begins P5 and then it has a 3 or 5 or even a 3Z or a 0Z after it. Go to **gov.uk** and search 'tax on pension lump sum'. That will give you all the options. Not that they try to make it difficult or anything!

The quickest way to sort it out is online. And to do that you will need a Government Gateway account. That should be easy to set up and is very handy as you will need it for all sorts of things. If you prefer you can fill in a paper form – best do that online and then print it out and post it.

It is worth the trouble? The average overpayment reclaimed is £2500 but if your pension fund is large, you may have paid tens of thousands of pounds too much tax. However, government figures imply that many do not bother or do not know about the overtaxing problem. Since pension freedom began in 2015, a total of £667 million of overpaid tax has been refunded to 262,000 people who have used the reclaim procedure. That is only one in 20 of the 1.5 million people who have cashed in their pot. Most of them will have been overtaxed on their money. So 19 out of 20 have not bothered to get it back. HMRC systems should work out the problem and repay them after the end of the tax year when it realises that the pension fund release was a one-off payment not a regular one. But that assumes HMRC gets its sums right at the right time – which I never do.

If you need help you can call HMRC's Taxes Helpline on 0300 200 3300, which is open from 8am to 8pm every day – except Sunday when it opens from 9am to 5pm. You will need to be patient. A cup of tea and a book might help. Calls are charged at normal rates so are probably free in your phone call bundle.

Now you have your money, we will see later what you might do with it.

Your DB pension

But what about those DB pensions? Just to make things more complicated there are two main sorts of DB pension. If your pension scheme is with a business, then it is what is called 'funded'. In other words, there is a big pot of money paid in over the years by the firm you work for and by you, all looked after by pension trustees, which will pay out the promised pensions. However, in the public sector the schemes are generally unfunded. They don't need a fund because they've got us – the taxpayers – to pay them. Unfunded schemes include civil servants, teachers, police officers and NHS staff. To confuse things, some of the public sector is funded – including the schemes for local authority workers, university lecturers and MPs.

If your pension is promised by an **unfunded** public sector scheme, then pension freedom does not apply to you. You cannot cash it in. So forget about it. And look forward to a good, index-linked pension underwritten by the government (aka the rest of us taxpayers). Move on to Chapter 9.

People in a **funded** DB scheme – the whole of the private sector and a few public sector schemes – can access the value of their pension fund. And for them it can be very tempting. They have a guaranteed pension, part of which at least is raised each year to reflect inflation (with a cap), and generally when they die their partner will get a smaller pension. To buy a pension like that would cost a fortune. So if you have one, it is very valuable and under pension freedom, you can take its value out of the pension fund. A pension of £10,000 a year can be worth £250,000 as a lump sum taken out of the fund. In some cases, it can be worth up to 40 times the annual pension. For most people, these are sums of money beyond their dreams.

So, if you transfer out of a pension fund you will get, say, £250,000 to put into your own pension pot and, if you choose, cash all or some of it in – though if you do that, tax would of course be due on three-quarters of it. People with an entitlement to a bigger pension will be able to convert it into a fund of half a million, a million, or more! Whoopee! But do not do it. Do not do it. Do not even think about doing it. It will almost always be a mistake.

Of course, the sharks are circling this massive honeypot (mixed metaphor alert). Some are vicious killers who will con you into letting them steal the fund. But most of the sharks are just chancers. And until very recently, it was very lucrative. You asked about cashing in your salary-related pension. The adviser asked for the details and explained the service was free – unless you moved it, when they would take a percentage of your fund – it varied but think 2% or even 3% in some cases. Which on a half-million-pound fund was ten grand at least. It was called contingent charging and, of course, set up a conflict of interest between you and the adviser. It was in their interest to recommend that you move, but usually not in your interest to do so. As a result, between the start of pension freedom and March 2020, 66 per cent of those given advice were advised to cash it in, more than 220,000 people.

The Financial Conduct Authority says that is bad advice for the majority of people. Financial advisers I know and trust reckon it is bad advice for 90 to 95 per cent. After several years of thinking, the FCA finally decided to ban contingent pricing and, since 1 October 2020, it should not happen. But if you have been badly advised in the past, you may want to consider making a complaint to your financial adviser for mis-advice. See page 173 in How to Complain.

Although these sums seem vast, they cannot and never will be able to buy you a pension like the one you have been promised. If your pension is worth more than £30,000, then by law you must get professional regulated financial advice. If it is worth less than that, or after the advice has been given, then your fund will be transferred to your own pension scheme. To transfer it you may want to set up a pension pot of your own – normally called a SIPP, which stands for – no, not Single Individual's Pension Pot, it is Self-Invested Personal Pension. Or you can transfer it to a pension fund run by an insurance company.

You can get £500 – from your pension fund – to help pay for financial advice about this transfer. But it is getting harder and harder to find a good independent financial adviser who will take on this compulsory pension advice role. Not least because insurance firms are getting very antsy about insuring them to give it. They fear expensive lawsuits if the advice turns out to be wrong. Which means those that do give this advice face a much higher premium. So many of them simply will not do it.

Although the advice in almost every case is not to do it, there are occasions when it might be a good idea:

- You have plenty of other pensions.
- This is a small pension and you need the cash now.
- You are very unwell and are not likely to live long enough to draw your pension for many years.

As I said earlier, good IFAs tell me maybe one in ten or twenty should be advised to do it. Make very sure you are one of those before you go ahead.

Beware investments abroad

One of the big ways that people have been conned out of their pension funds are foreign investments. Often with the word 'green' or nowadays 'sustainable' attached. They develop low-cost homes for workers. Or plant trees and harvest them. Or build a windfarm. Those are all cons that have robbed people of their pension savings over the last decade. Many of the developments are in South America. Even if you know a little about a country but nothing about the development, do not invest. Or, more briefly, if it is abroad, do not invest. To be fair, these investments do help some people. The thieves.

Alan Barratt and Susan Dalton persuaded 245 people to transfer out of their good final-salary pension schemes into criminal enterprises. They lost £13.7 million. The pair were sentenced to around five years each on 22 April 2022. The judge said they had caused misery to so many people. 'Each account I have read is a story of a life ruined,' he said. There are plenty of other similar examples.

Small pensions

There are special and, needless to say, complex rules about very small pensions – trivial pensions as they call them. These probably will give a pension of not more that £400 or £500 a year and are worth up to £10,000. You may be able to take it straight out of a defined benefit pension scheme without all the hassle of moving it first. It applies only to salary-related pensions – DB as they like to call them.

There is a lot more to the rules about trivial commutation and small pots. One brief guide I know is eight pages long, not eight lines. Ask your pension scheme or, if you have one, your IFA about this.

You can get good clear advice free from the MoneyHelper service – perhaps under its older brands Pension Wise 0800 138 3944 or the Pensions Advisory Service 0800 011 3797.

USING THE MONEY

When you get your pension pot and the time has come when you want to call it a day, then what do you do with your £250,000 or £25,000?

The more money you have in your pot, the more choices you have. If you have £5 in your bank account or £500,000, you are free to spend it how you like. But with a bigger sum, you have more choice.

Annuities

I've talked before about insurance being a gamble. Annuities are the ultimate punt – a bet on your own life. You give the insurance company a lot of money. In exchange, it promises you an income for life. Let's say you have £133,333 and you take your 25% tax-free lump sum to do what you want with, leaving you a neat £100,000. You give that £100,000 to an insurance company. In exchange, it promises you an income for life. Whenever you die, it keeps the whole of the £100,000. It hopes you die quite soon. You hope you will live a very long time. If you do, then you will be paid a lot more than the money you put in.

On the insurer's side are – you guessed it – the actuaries. They know that a 65-year-old can expect to live 21 years. By which I mean – averaged between men and women – half of us will die younger and half older. Annuities, like all forms of insurance, are banned by law from discriminating between men and women. It will also invest the money you gave it.

There are choices you can make to increase – or reduce – the amount you get. Be honest about your health. If you have any health condition that will reduce your life expectancy, tell the insurer. Are you diabetic? Do you have angina, high blood pressure? Have you had a stroke or a tumour? None of these is good news of course, but it will mean you get a bigger annuity. Also, tell the insurer if you smoke or drink heavily. If so, the chances are you will probably die younger than average, so you will get a higher annuity. In the past, many insurers (and even worse some advisers) have failed to explain the importance of considering your health when buying an annuity.

Then decide if:

> ***You want your spouse or civil partner to get the income if you die before them. You can opt for them to get half or two-thirds of it. That will reduce the annuity you get.***
>
> ***You want a guaranteed period when the income will be paid even if you die very early in the deal. That may not reduce your income much.***
>
> ***You want your income to go up each year to try to match inflation. If so, your annuity will be much lower at the start.***

As I write, that £100,000 you have saved up will buy a 65-year-old, single, healthy, non-smoker with no pension for a partner an annual income for life of £7402 a year, or £616 a month, which does not rise with inflation. After 14 years, you will more than break even but the insurance company will have won because of the investment growth. If you live longer, you're quids in. However, if you choose an annuity that rises with inflation capped at 5% a year, you will get just £4301 in the first year and then more each year depending on inflation. If inflation averages 4% a year, it will take 14 years before your pension is £7402. And you will be 99 before you have had as much from your index-linked pension as from your flat-rate one. These figures were correct in October 2022. They may well be different when you read this. Check at **comparison.moneyhelper.org.uk/en/guaranteed-income-for-life/quotes** and go to a broker for accurate best-buy quotes.

And remember that you will also have your state pension, which will be around £10,000 a year and is protected against inflation. So although index-linking seems a good idea, it may not be for a minority of your income.

Drawdown

When you learnt your pension pot was £100,000, you probably looked forward to a good retirement. But at best it can bring you less than half the state pension index-linked. It is for this reason that people want an alternative. And when that happens, the financial services industry usually steps in with an even more expensive solution! It is called drawdown. You keep your pension fund. Take your quarter tax-free cash and the rest goes into drawdown. All that word means is that you take out money from your invested pension pot either regularly or as and when you need it.

Drawdown funds are supposed to concentrate on investments that bring in income, so you can draw that without taking too much of your capital. So if your £100,000 earns 3% return – which it might – then you can have £3000 a year from it – which is taxable. And the £100,000 is still intact. Yes. But don't forget investments can go down as well as plummet. So after a few years, your £100,000 may be worth a lot less – or of course a lot more. Over the last few years, the value of investments, particularly in the USA, has soared. Realistically your investment will probably, after charges, yield more like 2%, ignoring whether the capital is depleted or not. And IFAs will do complex calculations for you about taking money out, which is part what the fund has earned and part spending the capital and how that might be calculated to eke out the fund so that it is empty at the same moment you die.

But remember that you do not need an even income over your retired life. You need more when you are newly retired and fit and active and a lot less when you are waiting for that

100th birthday telegram from King Charles III or it may even be William V.

One variation on this is called flexible access drawdown. It is very clever. And of most use for people who have bigger amounts than £100,000.

So, let us say you have £240,000. You say to your IFA you want an income of £10,000 a year. So in year one they take out of your pot £40,000. £10,000 is tax-free (a quarter of every drawn amount is tax-free). You get that paid over the year as a tax-free income of £833 a month. The remaining £30,000 can stay in the fund or can go into the SIPP provider's bank account for you to use as and when you need it. When you do need it, then it will be taxed. But forget about it for now.

Next year, another £40,000 is taken out. Rather sweetly the official word for it is 'crystallisation'. As before, £10,000 is paid to you over the year. The other £30,000 stays where it was, but it is crystallised rather than uncrystallised money. The same happens for each of the next four years, by which time your entire fund has been crystallised and you have had a quarter of it paid to you – £60,000 over six years tax-free income. And there is £180,000 left (plus whatever investment growth there has been or, of course, minus whatever investment loss there has been). You then take that at £10,000 a year over the next 18 years and it is taxable income now, but never mind because you now pay basic rate tax so it is not too bad. You get £8000 a year net. Which is still OK. And, assuming neither growth nor loss, that lasts you another 18 years. By which time it comes to an end. You are 89 and slowing down, so you do not really need as much income anymore.

If your fund is substantial, do take advice from an independent financial adviser (see page 206 in Investing for how to find one). And ask about flexible drawdown. If you do not take advice, then the firm running it is supposed to present you with simple to understand choices – now called 'Investment Pathways' – and to keep charges below 0.75% a year. The financial services industry is remarkably skilled at finding ways round rules, especially those relating to charges, so check the small print of what is really going on.

Trigger events

You can continue paying.into a pension up to the age of 75. So there is more on that in Chapter 9. However, be aware that decisions made now can limit what you can put into a pension. Once you initiate what is called 'a trigger event', the amount you can save into a pension plummets from £40,000 a year to £4000 (and it can never be more than your annual earnings). A trigger event is almost any of the things in this chapter that involve taking money out of your pension fund. The only thing that is not is simply taking your tax-free lump sum (which the pension industry abbreviates to PCLS – answer at the end of the chapter if you can't guess). Anything else, however modest and small, is a trigger event, collapsing your annual allowance by 90 per cent. Ask your adviser about this before you take money out.

Of course £40,000 a year into a pension will be beyond the dreams of the average person and even £4000 may still seem enormous – you put in £266 a month and the Chancellor tops it up to £333 – but do beware of unwittingly pulling that trigger.

Invest it yourself

Of course, you can do other things. Take out the whole lot and invest it yourself or keep it in a deposit account. Hint – keep the charges down. Just because you are ancient, and this is an ex-pension fund, does not mean you get any special treatment. It is up to you where to invest and what to do with the income produced (if any) and how to live on the fund for your remaining years. It might be great, it might be a disaster. But at least you were in charge of it.

Keep it in cash

Some people will choose to keep their pension pot in cash. It is probably a silly thing to do but there are billions – high billions – languishing in cash. These people look at things this way:

- I don't trust the financial services industry.
- I have heard charges for investing it are very high and risks are great.
- I want to be in control.
- I could not bear it if I woke up one morning and the stock market had crashed and taken away the money for my old age.

I have great sympathy with that view. But you will struggle to find a financial adviser to agree with you.

If you want your money in cash **make sure it is in real cash** – not some cash fund that pays you less than the charges it takes. They are a scam – and yes I do know they are run by some of the most respectable insurance firms! I still say they are a scam on the unwary. Put it in the best paying deposit account you can. Remember this is long-term money – it has to last you 20 years or more. So some can be locked up for five years if you want, while some should be in easy-access accounts to give you, well, easy access to it.

Do the arithmetic

Let's say your pension pot is £100,000. Find out your life expectancy from ONS.gov.uk – search 'life expectancy calculator'. Say it is 20 years, then you can take £5000 a year out. But beware. There is a one in four chance you will live nearly 30 years and a one in ten chance it will be more than that. So be prepared to take less out as you get older.

My experience of old old age is that past a certain time people do want to do less and live a narrower life than they do in their 60s or 70s. So do not obsess about having the same amount each year. You will need less as age creeps up on you.

Of course, the great wealth killer is inflation. It has been low for a generation. But in late 2021, it started to soar. If high rates of inflation persist and interest paid on savings does not rise with it, then when you take out your last £5000 it many well only buy a third or less of what your first £5000 would buy.

So cash has that risk. Inflation affects invested money too, but the hope is it will grow more than cash and at least partly offset inflation. That is the hope.

All that was a bit long and complex – don't blame me, I didn't invent the pension rules!! So here's a quick reminder.

Remember

- From age 55 you can cash in most pensions – but it may not be a good idea.
- But you cannot cash it in if you are in a public sector pension, like the NHS, teachers, police etc..

- If your pension is related to your salary, it may seem to be worth an enormous amount but it is almost never a good idea to cash it in. You will usually need to get professional advice and that may be difficult to find.
- If you have a pension pot it is easy – normally you can just ask for it.
- If you cash in your pension:
  - You will pay too much tax – ask for it back as soon as possible.
  - A quarter will be tax-free.
  - Never, ever invest it in any scheme that is being promoted, especially if it is abroad – you could lose the lot.

INHERITANCE TAX

Do not be afraid of inheritance tax (IHT). First, it is paid after you are dead. Second, someone else pays it. Almost the perfect tax for me! Joking aside (was I joking? Hmmm), around one in 16 estates will pay inheritance tax this year. So if you see a funeral passing and people are weeping, 94 per cent of the time they are not lamenting the tax they will have to pay. Despite that, it is still probably the least popular tax, with a quarter of the population saying they hate it. Only council tax comes close.

It is of course understandable that you want to leave something for your children (if you have them) or the home for rescued donkeys (if you don't). But although we've never met, I would rather you spent your money having a good time while you were alive than worrying how much the Chancellor might get after you have died. And I expect your children would too (if not, do they deserve anything? Discuss).

Warning: Inheritance tax rules can get a bit tricky. Especially when words are limited. So concentrate, please. And if you have substantial assets, talk to a specialist lawyer about the tax that may be due.

Warning 2: These rules and allowances were correct in 2022 but may change in the future.

Dodging it (legally)

When you die, your assets are added up, your bills paid and the balance is called your 'estate'. If it is less than a certain amount, no inheritance tax is due. That amount has been frozen for many years at £325,000 and may stay there for some time yet. It is called the 'nil-rate band'. Even if your estate is above that amount, no tax may be due for three reasons:

- Everything you leave to your spouse or civil partner is completely free of IHT. There is zilch to pay. So, if you are in legal couplage, that is usually the best thing to do.
- If you own the home you live in and you leave it to a direct descendant, its value up to another £175,000 residence band can be added to that threshold, making £500,000. Direct means a child(ren), grandchild, great-grandchild etc.. Sorry nieces, siblings and fourth cousins twice removed, you don't count. However, 'child' does include adopted, fostered, and step-children and their spouses or civil partners.
- If you are a widow/er and your spouse left everything to you, then when you die you have in effect their allowances too. So, a basic £650,000 threshold and a residence band of up to £350,000, making £1,000,000 in theory altogether. That magic million was done to fulfil a promise made by former Chancellor of the Exchequer George Osborne that he would exempt estates up to a

million pounds. Which he did. Sort of, in some limited circumstances!

Note that the residence band is up to those amounts. So, if the home you pass down is less than the maximum, you only get the home's value. But if you lived in a home but then downsized, you can count the value of the more expensive home. It gets complicated then so your heirs should seek advice. If the home is worth more than £2 million, the exemption is tapered away.

Gifts

If your estate is likely to be above those amounts and you don't have a spouse or civil partner to leave things to, then you can make gifts that reduce your estate up to certain limits. These haven't changed for years either.

Gifts you make more than seven years before you die are ignored completely. They just do not count as part of your estate, however large they are. However, before you get any bright ideas, there is a trap called GROB. Gifts with reservation of benefit. Many have fallen down this trap and their heirs end up paying large amounts of tax. Suppose you have a Picasso painting and you give it to your daughter with a legal document making her the owner. If it still hangs in your home, that doesn't count as giving it away. It is a GROB. More likely, you give your house to your children but continue to live in it, then it is counted as your property not theirs. You can get round that if you pay them a market rent but then they will be liable for tax on that income and for capital gains tax when they sell it, so it is not a good idea. Also, if they get divorced or go bankrupt or just decide they don't like you anymore, they can make you leave your own home.

Some smaller gifts do not count, even if you do die within seven years.

You can give away up to £3000 each tax year without it counting at all. If you gave away nothing the year before, you can bring that forward and give £6000. These allowances are personal so a couple can give away double those amounts. And if they are married or CP'd, one can give the other the money first if need be. This £3000 is the total you can give away to one or more individuals – it is not £3000 to each of your children, for example. If there are three children, it is £1000 each.

If there is a wedding during the tax year, then you can give up to £5,000 to a child of yours as a wedding gift and up to £2,500 to a grandchild (or great-grandchild) or £1,000 to anyone else. They are all conditional on the marriage taking place. They are on top of the £3000 allowances and again are personal, so partners can do double that.

In addition, you can give away gifts of up to £250 to any number of people – though not the same ones who got a gift under the other exemptions.

Less well known are gifts out of income. If your income is more than you need to live the lifestyle you choose, then any excess can be given away without it counting as a gift. This can be very useful for perhaps an ageing widow with more than adequate pensions.

Oddly, you are under no obligation to write down any gifts you make but it will certainly help your executors if you do so, especially gifts from income, explaining with arithmetic showing the excess income that you do not need.

Other exempt gifts are money for maintenance to an ex-spouse (or ex-CP), gifts to maintain your children (but not grandchildren etc.) while they are in full-time education, and gifts to any relative (even those second cousins once removed) if they are financially dependent on you.

But, I hear you say, wealthy people are renowned for not paying inheritance tax – how do they do it? They spend a lot of money maintaining a trust. But they are fraught with problems too. Unless your home is very valuable and way above the limits where inheritance tax would be due – and remember that can be up to £1 million on the second parent's death – then it is usually a waste of money. See the DO NOT TOUCH box below.

Life insurance

If you have a life insurance policy that pays out on your death, then the payment can form part of your estate. To avoid that, you can ask the insurance company to make the policy 'written in trust'. That means instead of going directly to your dependants via your estate, the money is paid into a trust, which then passes it on to your dependants. That two-step process avoids the proceeds counting as part of your estate. However, like most wheezes, this is being squeezed by legal changes and if the insurance pay-out is more than £325,000, it may not be worth it. Ask your insurer's advice.

Inheriting your pension

If you have a pension fund of your own like a SIPP or a personal pension, then that should definitely be made so that it passes to your heirs on your death. That bypasses the estate and IHT too. If you die before the age of 75, then your heirs can have the whole fund tax-free and spend it tax-free too. If you are over 75 when you die, then they can put it into their own pension fund and pay no charges. They can then take it out under the same rules that apply to individuals taking money out of their own pension fund – see page 220.

DO NOT TOUCH – Tax avoidance schemes

Some financial consultants and even insurance companies have made a lot of money selling people plans to reduce or avoid inheritance tax. These schemes juggle the ownership of money or a home and making gifts into or from Trusts – and often involve taking out an insurance policy as well. They are often designed principally to generate commission for the person who sells them. If the scheme does not work it is your heirs, not the adviser, who will end up paying the bill.

In 2005, the government clamped down on one kind of scheme, leaving 30,000 people, who had paid good money for advice, with a tax bill every year just to carry on living in their own home. Fifteen years ago, the government changed the rules to make such schemes more expensive. In 2013, a new General Anti-Abuse Rule (GARR) came into force that makes it even harder to set up cunning schemes to avoid tax. So, generally, these plans are best avoided.

Even if they work, it is not just you who will have to spend money. Your heirs may find they face charges too to take property out of a trust and enjoy it themselves. If you want to consider one, then before you commit yourself make sure it has the positive approval of HM Revenue & Customs and discuss it with an impartial professional adviser – such as a solicitor or accountant – who you have found yourself and who is entirely separate from the company or individual selling the product. And unless you have an estate valued in the millions, it is not worth the risk.

THE STATE PENSION

Ever since 1909, people who worked have been given a pension when they reached a certain age. It has changed over the years from 70 in 1909, to 65 for men and 60 for women in 1940, then it slowly started creeping up for women, then going up more quickly for women, until it was 65, then up again to 66 for both for anyone born from 6 October 1954. It will rise again to 67 for those born from 6 April 1961. After that it may increase further.

Once you reach that age, you can claim your state pension. It is £185.15 a week or £9627.80 a year. For the next couple of years at least, it is guaranteed to go up each April by at least 2.5% and in fact rather more this coming April. After that the rules may change, but it will almost certainly go up in line with prices and may go up in line with wages. It is a good deal.

That is what is called the new state pension. It began from April 2016 for anyone reaching state pension from that date. That was women born 6 April 1953 or later and men born 6 April 1951 and later. So all men and women in this chapter. Before that, the pension was different. **If you were born before those dates, then look at the next chapter to find out about your state pension.**

To get the full new state pension, you must have at least 35 years of National Insurance contributions either by:

- Working and paying them.
- Getting credits if you:
  - » Got child benefit for a child under 12 (it used to be under 16).
  - » Registered as unemployed.
  - » Claimed certain benefits, like carer's allowance or employment and support allowance.

Sometimes 35 years is not enough. If you paid into a good salary-related scheme at work, your new state pension will be reduced. You can get rid of that reduction by paying extra National Insurance contributions – beyond the 35 years – from 6 April 2016 by either:

- Working and earning enough to pay them.

OR

- Paying them voluntarily.

Paying them voluntarily is a very good deal and worth doing if your pension is reduced for this reason. My blog explains it all, I hope clearly – **paullewismoney.blogspot.com** and search 'target 185'. Karen was one of several who tweeted me after my April 2022 update of that blog:

> *'Thank you so much for such an excellent and comprehensive explanation of the unnecessarily complex rules.'*
>
> *Karen, via Twitter*

If you have fewer than 35 years of contributions, then you may be able to buy extra now to fill past gaps. The rules change on 6 April 2023 so look into it now if you need them. Find out more at **gov.uk** and search 'voluntary national insurance'. Or check my blog **paullewismoney.blogspot.com** and search 'fill that gap'.

> *'Thanks to your promotion my wife has received her back payment (£2976.42p) and her pension has been increased to the level of roughly 60% of mine based on my NIC contributions, which are 'complete'. Effectively up from £38.81p to £82.73p, which is massively of benefit to us.'*
>
> *Ian, via email*

State pension and tax

Your state pension forms part of your taxable income. But it is paid to you gross without any tax being deducted. And that can have peculiar effects on your other income. If you still work or have a work pension or annuity payment coming in and you pay tax, then when you reach state pension age and claim your pension the tax on your other income will go up. This tax shocks, puzzles – and annoys – people.

The Chancellor collects the tax due on your state pension by taking more off your other income. You will recall (and if not, it is on page 111 in Chapter 5) that your tax code represents the tax-free income you can have in the year. Normally, that amount is £12,570 a year and your tax code is 1257L (go on, read page 111 again). That is used to take the tax off your pension or earnings. When you claim your state pension, your tax code is reduced.

If your state pension is £9628 then that uses up most of your tax-free allowance (£12,570 – £9628 = £2942). So, the rest of your income above £2942 is taxed and your tax code is reduced to 294L. So you pay more tax on the remaining income because, with your state pension, you have a higher income and the tax is all taken from that other income.

One other peculiar fact about your state pension and tax. The amount you actually receive is not taxed. Tax is taken according to how much you should receive in the tax year. That normally makes little or no difference. But if there is an underpayment when you first claim with arrears paid later, then you may be taxed on them early. You should always check your tax each year to see if it seems correct.

Retire later

A couple of months before state pension age you will get a letter inviting you to claim your state pension. You do not have to claim it. If you do not need it then, it may be worth delaying it – especially if you pay higher rate tax now but when you leave work and claim your pension you will pay a lower rate of tax. Delaying your claim also means that the pension will be more when you do claim it. It is increased by 1% for every nine weeks you delay. So if you delay 52 weeks, you will get a pension that is 5.8% higher. The extra percentage applies to all the parts of your pension but when pensions go up each April, the extra will increase only with inflation, which may be less than the rise in the rest of the pension.

If you delay five years, then your pension will be raised by more than a quarter (28.9%). If you do not need your pension this can seem like a good deal. But the enhancement has been carefully worked out to be neutral – in other words, an average person will get the same amount of pension before they die if they live to a typical age of around 86. So, again it is a gamble on your life – this time You v. the Government Actuary (yes, there really is one!). So if you expect to have a shorter life than normal due to illness or smoking, it is probably not worth doing. If you expect to live longer, then it is. But, I say again, paying higher rate tax before pension age and basic rate tax after can tip the balance heavily in favour of doing it. As the Bellman said:

'Just the place for a Snark! I have said it thrice:

What I tell you three times is true.'

Also, and less poetically, it is a slightly better bet for women because you live longer.

Remember

- You are entitled to a state pension once you reach 66.
- If your pension is less than the full amount, look in to paying extra National Insurance contributions to boost it.
- State pension is taxable but always paid without tax being deducted – so other income will be taxed more to cover the tax due on it.
- If you don't need your pension at 66 it may be worth not claiming it until you do – it will be increased for each nine weeks you defer it.

BENEFITS AS YOU GET OLDER

It is a strange fact of life, or at least the benefits system (never confuse the two), that at the age of 65 years 11 months you need £77 a week to live. But as you turn 66 and 1 hour, you need £182 a week. Also at 65 years 11 months, you only need a fraction of your rent paid and, in England but not in Scotland or Wales, you will have to pay at least 20 per cent of your council tax and your benefit will be cut if you have more bedrooms than you need. At the age of 66 and one hour, you may get all your rent paid, all your council tax, and you can have eight bedrooms if you wish. But be aware, if you are part of a couple you both have to be over 66.

The moment you turn 66, the state pension age, your needs are seen as completely different. Especially in England – some of the rules are different in Scotland, Wales and Northern Ireland, where they either pass their own laws or implement what they call 'mitigating provisions'.

Here are the sums. A single person who has very little or no income the month before they reach the age of 66 is deemed by the state to need £77 a week to live on. To get that they must usually spend 35 hours a week looking for work. Leaving aside their rent – another long story – that is all they will get from universal credit unless they are disabled. The moment they reach the grand old age of 66, they can no longer claim universal credit. If their state pension is not enough, they must get another benefit called pension credit. That is more than twice as much – £182.60 a week – and they do not have to do anything for it. All things being equal, they can claim that for the rest of their life. You may notice that it is less than the standard rate of the new state pension (£185.15 a week). So only people with a reduced state pension at 66 will be able to get it. However, it is considerably more than the basic state pension that older pensioners get – £141.85 a week. As a result, nearly one-and-a-half million older pensioners – by which I mean women born before 6 April 1953 and men before 6 April 1951 – also claim pension credit. More on them in the next chapter.

All these amounts are correct until the start of April 2023 but after that will certainly be higher.

Universal credit and pension credit are means-tested, so if you have other income they will be reduced. They will also be reduced if your savings exceed £6000 (universal credit) or £10,000 (pension credit). And if you have more than £16,000, you will not get universal credit at all but you may still get a reduced amount of pension credit.

Welcome to the complexity of the benefit system! And we have not scratched the surface of it yet.

Claim it

Although the rules are complex, claiming pension credit is simple once you are 66. You just call 0800 99 1234. But nearly a million people over pension age have not done that yet. There is £57 a week extra on average just sitting there waiting for you. This money came from the taxes you and everyone else paid – and remember even if you don't work you pay tax when you buy things – so it is only fair and right that you get it now.

If you are over 70, the rules about pension credit are a bit more complex but that is the price you pay for them being a bit more generous – actually none of it is generous but you know what I mean. Details of that are in the next chapter.

CASHING IN YOUR HOME

Are you sitting in a fortune? If you own your home, it is probably worth a small lottery win. But your income is probably not as big as you would like – is it ever? Well, now you are 55 you can cash in your home. I do not recommend it at 55. I barely recommend it at 65. That is why I explain it in full in the next chapter on page 255. By the time you turn that page, you will be old enough.

OVER-50S LIFE INSURANCE

One thing you will be heavily sold at your age as a 50-plus-year-old is life insurance. As I say on page 160 in Chapter 6, I only recommend life insurance for those with financial dependants or a joint mortgage. There is not really any point to it otherwise. But some older celebs who should know better – especially the numerate ones – earn a living promoting 'over-50s life insurance'. They are obviously better at counting the money they earn from doing that than working out the odds of this life insurance gamble. Because – like all insurance – it IS a gamble. You are betting against professionals who have been doing it for more than 200 years. And the House always wins.

Without going into all the arithmetic, one heavily advertised scheme charges a 65-year-old £20 a month and promises their heirs £4091 on their death. Most people will pay into the scheme more than they get out of it. That is especially true for women, who generally live longer than men.

Typically, a woman will pay premiums for four years after she has paid in what her family will get out – and waste £1189.

And you cannot just stop paying in when you reach the breakeven point. Your heirs will then get nothing. Yep. The insurer will keep all you have paid in and give them nothing. And before you ask, yes that is legal. In some circumstances, it *may* be worth cancelling the policy. If the future premiums add up to less than they will get when you pop off – assume you are average – then do not give it up. Forget about all the premiums you have paid before. The shorter the time you have paid in, the more likely it is that you should give up. But it is still a gamble on your date of death.

These policies should be avoided. Whatever your age, the House wins most of the time.

One big attraction of these plans is:

NO MEDICAL NEEDED!!!

There are not even any questions about your health. If you die within the first year (the first two years with some insurers), your heirs only get back your premiums. That is the zero on the roulette wheel. But if you live beyond that and are a heavy smoker or have a medical condition, that will reduce your life expectancy to well below the average. So, one of these plans may be worthwhile. You are going into the casino with some marked cards. But remember you are gambling against professionals. They wear T-shirts printed with 'Been there. Seen it. Done them.' Overall, the House wins. Always.

QUIZ ANSWER: PCLS stands for Pension Commencement Lump Sum.

CHAPTER 9

WOUND DOWN 70–99

It is not the final curtain but it is the final phase. That may start later than 70 and it may end earlier than 99. But this is when you have wound down. All that mad work and commuting, or looking for a job, struggling on benefits, paying off a mortgage, worrying about children, if you had them, all that may be behind you – or, of course, it may not. Retirement should be a long holiday at the end of your life. But for many, it is not.

THE OLD STATE PENSION

Generally, women aged 70 or more in 2023 and men aged 72 or more will get the old state pension. That's because the new state pension began for men born 6 April 1951 or later and women born 6 April 1953 or later. If you want to be jealous, go back to Chapter 8 where the new one is explained.

The new and the old state pensions are very different as is the extra help you can get if your pension is not enough. This chapter is about the old state pension paid to the people born before those dates.

It comes in several bits. The basic state pension is currently £141.85 a week (£7376.20 a year) and on top of that there may be two extras:

- A tiddly bit called **graduated retirement benefit**. It is based on earnings from 1961 to 1975 and averages just over £4 a week.
- A much bigger bit called **additional pension** – we used to call it SERPS when it was introduced by Labour's Barbara Castle in 1978. It is related to your earnings, so the more you earned the bigger it is. The average additional pension is £34 a week but for some it can be much more – even bigger than the basic pension itself for people who earned well.

The additional pension you have earned may be reduced if at some stage you paid into a good pension scheme at work. By 'good', I mean one of those that pay a pension related to your salary (a so-called DB scheme). This will result in a deduction from your additional pension. That is because while you were in that salary scheme, you paid a slightly lower rate of National Insurance contributions and your work pension scheme is supposed to pay you at least as much as the additional pension deducted. They always will. However, people who paid into a personal pension in the 1980s and 1990s and 'contracted out' of SERPS may also have a deduction and there is no guarantee that the personal pension will make up for the loss. It was one of the first great pension mis-selling scandals. It won't be the last.

It is important to separate in your mind the basic state pension and these earnings-related parts. The basic state pension rises each year according to what is called the triple lock – earnings or prices (as at the previous September) but with a minimum rise of 2.5%. There was a government promise that the triple lock guarantee will last until April 2026 but it was watered down for the April 2022 rise and it may be changed again for the worse. As I write it is still not completely clear how much it will rise in April 2023 and, in the long-term, the triple lock may go. Traditionally, the additional and graduated bits only rise with inflation as does any extra pension you get (called increments) for deferring it. That may change in the future.

PENSION CREDIT

There are probably two-and-a-half million people over pension age whose income is below what we might call the poverty line. In other words, their income is lower than the minimum the government says people of that age need to live. But less than one-and-a-half million claim extra money through pension credit. The other million could claim an average of £37 a week but don't.

I have been writing about the mystery of why this missing million do not claim for many, many years. And the government has occasionally tried to encourage claims, most recently in the summer of 2022.

Here's a rough guide. And remember this version of pension credit is only for people who get the old state pension, which is men born before 6 April 1951 and women born before 6 April 1953. Remember too that these amounts are all correct until the start of April 2023 but after that will certainly be higher.

Pension credit comes in two parts.

- **Guarantee credit**, which makes your income up to £182.60 a week or £278.70 for a couple. But note, if you are a couple and making a first claim for pension credit, both of you need to be over state pension age. Note too that couple here means a couple who live together as if they were married, whether they are or not.
- The second part is called **savings credit**, though it has nothing to do with savings. It is simply a little extra money, up to £14.48 a week (£16.20 for a couple), if you have an income that is above £158 for a single person or £252 for a couple. This extra help is phased out as income rises, but it does mean that you can get some pension credit – just a penny or two – with an income as high as £218 a week (single) or £319 (couple). Why should you claim a few pence of help? Because once you reach 75 that few pence will entitle you to a free TV licence worth £159. It can also act as a gateway to other things. Like a 100 per cent discount on your council tax.

If you are disabled or a carer, you may be able to get pension credit with higher incomes than these. But if you have savings over £10,000, the income at which you can get pension credit will be reduced. If your head aches with all these numbers, the easiest thing to do is to call 0800 99 1234 and claim your pension credit. Nearly a million people who could get it, don't. I hope this book means you won't be one of them.

If you want to check privately if you are entitled to pension credit, you can find out from the website **entitledto.co.uk**. I recommended that to *Money Box* listener Valerie who was 75 years old and living alone – she told me she had been confused by the government website, had taken my advice and emailed me this:

> *'Hi Paul*
>
> *Many thanks for your reply to my query, and it will be worth my while making an application.*
>
> *Your help is appreciated. I am a regular* Money Box *listener.*
>
> *Regards*
>
> *Valerie'*
>
> *Valerie, via email*

ATTENDANCE ALLOWANCE

As we get older, aches and pains can turn into disabilities and it is important to remember that older people aged at least 66 can get more money if they need help from another person to live their lives safely and comfortably.

The benefit is called attendance allowance and is up to £89.60 a week. It is paid to people who are severely disabled and need care from someone else. Their disability can be physical or mental but must be severe. The key thing is they need help. It does not matter whether they actually get help – though they normally will of course. Nor does it matter who gives it – the council, a paid person, a relative, a partner. You can claim when you need the help but there is a six-month wait before you qualify.

The rules can seem complicated but the main qualification is that you need help from someone else. That can be in connection with your bodily functions, such as eating, washing, dressing, seeing, hearing, and using the toilet. Or it can be to keep you safe – someone to watch over you to keep you out of danger, whether that is falling or hurting yourself.

If you need help by day AND by night, you get £89.60 a week. If you need it by day OR by night, there is a lower rate of £60 a week. These rates will almost certainly rise in April 2023.

Attendance allowance is tax-free and not means-tested – you can get it regardless of your income or other resources. Other benefits you get already may increase once you get it. About one in nine pensioners get attendance allowance. But that proportion has been falling – twelve years ago it was one in six – so there may be many more people who could get it if they claimed. The person looking after you may be able to get carer's allowance of £67.60 a week but that is not paid on top of their state pension.

> ***'Dear Paul It took some time to wade through the paperwork but it was worth the effort and this morning we received a letter that we had been awarded the higher rate of attendance allowance backdated to last month. What a relief. It will make such a difference to us.***
>
> ***We can't thank you enough.'***
>
> ***Christine, via email***

More information:

- **independentage.org** – search 'attendance allowance' or call 0330 021 2503.

- **gov.uk** – search 'attendance allowance' or call 0800 731 0122; in Northern Ireland 0800 587 0912.

SPENDING THE HOUSE

If you are at least 70 and short of cash, why not spend a bit of your home? By that I mean borrowing money against it and not paying that money back until after you die, when of course your heirs will have to pay it out of your estate. It is called 'equity release' – like many financial terms it seems to have been thought up by people who do not want anyone to understand what they are talking about.

It works like this. Suppose your home is worth £150,000. You borrow £50,000 to spend and promise to pay that back plus interest when you die or go into a care home. For a couple that happens when the second one dies or goes into a care home. While you are alive it costs you nothing. You have 'released' some of the value (or 'equity') in your home while you are still alive rather than leaving the whole lot to children who probably do not need it anyway. Win-win.

Well, sort of. In the past, equity release had a well-deserved reputation for being bad value. The interest rate on the mortgage you took out was high and was fixed and nowadays seems extraordinary; there were penalties if you paid off the debt early; and it was difficult to move – the schemes were not portable if you downsized – or upsized come to that. Nowadays, some of those problems have been solved but you have to think carefully if it is the right answer for you. And to help you do that, the law now says you have to take professional advice from a financial adviser with a specialist equity release qualification. Only ever go to a firm that is independent and looks at the whole market for you. And only ever consider using a firm that is a member of the Equity Release Council.

Each year, interest is added to the money you have taken out. But you do not pay the interest. Instead, it is added to the loan. The next year you pay interest on the whole lot including the interest from the previous year. That is called compound interest (see page 55 in Chapter 4) and it can build up the debt substantially. In the past, the interest rates charged on equity release were high and the total owed grew very rapidly. But nowadays competition and falling interest rates generally have meant that the interest charged on equity release is similar to that charged on a standard mortgage used to buy a home.

As I write, rates are around 6% or 7%. By the time you read this, they may be higher. At 6% your debt will double every 12 years, so if you borrow £10,000 and live 20 years then the debt from your estate will be approximately £32,000 – more than treble what you borrowed. During that time of course house prices will probably also have risen – Nationwide says over the last 20 years they have increased 173%. Of course, that may not be true over the next 20 years but there should still be plenty left for your family to inherit.

Now, you may be wondering what if I live a long time and the debt gets bigger than the value of my home? In the past that was a real problem. Now it is not because all reputable lenders give you a guarantee that will not happen. The debt can only be as big as the home is worth. That is why I said earlier that you must only ever use a firm that belongs to the Equity Release Council, who all give that 'no negative equity' guarantee.

You can reduce the impact of compound interest by taking a drawdown scheme (it is a confusing name because it is different from a pension drawdown). You agree to borrow that £50,000 but instead of doing it all at once, you take the first £10,000 and then draw the rest as and when you need it. You only pay interest on the money you have actually drawn down.

One thing you do not have to do is ask – or even tell – the kids. Though of course it is probably better to do so and to involve them in the decision. But remember it is your home and you can do what you like with it. Most children would rather you used the money locked up in your home to give yourself a fun and easy retirement. And if they don't? Well, do it anyway, it is your money not theirs.

The amount you can release will depend on your age and health. At 55 it is only around a quarter of the value of your home. So, on a £200,000 home you can raise £50,000. It rises about ten percentage points per decade, so at 65 it is about 35 per cent or a bit more. Then 45 per cent at 75 and once you reach 85 or over, it is 55 per cent. If you are unwell and your health or habits – such as smoking – mean you are likely to die early (sorry to be blunt!) it will be more. It is the age and health of the younger partner that counts. I never recommend it at 55. At 65 it is OK. At 70 plus it is better value.

You can use the money for anything you like.

- Urgent things like paying off an interest-only mortgage or an expensive credit card debt. That can help you sleep at night.
- Practical things like a modern kitchen or bathroom to make life easier day-by-day or a garden makeover to reduce the need to bend or kneel too much.
- Luxuries like a new car or perhaps a caravan.
- Generous things like giving your kids some of their inheritance early to help them buy a home.
- Fun things like a special holiday – on safari or up a mountain or a luxury cruise.

Remember, it is your money. You worked hard to buy that home. Never feel guilty about spending it before it is too late.

Some homes will never, or usually not, be accepted by the schemes:

- former council property and housing developments aimed at retired people – usually not
- leasehold flats with less than 75 years on the lease – never
- freehold flats – usually not
- flats with cladding issues – never
- mobile homes, sometimes called park homes – never
- houseboats – never
- a building that is not standard construction – never
- properties outside the UK – never

You can move as long as the new home is acceptable to the lender.

If you have savings in the bank, use those first before you think of equity release. If you get a means-tested benefit such as pension credit or council tax reduction or, if you are under pension age, universal credit or tax credits, then borrowing the money will normally stop the benefit. So, it will seldom be worthwhile.

MARRIAGE ALLOWANCE

Another way to have a bit more money is to check your tax. And particularly if you are married and one of you pays tax and the other doesn't. One of the gripes people send me is about the personal tax allowance – the income you can have before any tax is due, which is currently £12,570. The gripe is this: my wife doesn't work and can't now because she is unwell. Why can't I have her allowance so I pay less tax on my income that keeps the two of us?

It's a fair point and there is a partial – very partial – solution. You can transfer some of your personal allowance – only a tenth – of it to your spouse and that tenth is rounded up to £1260. That reduces the tax paid by the taxpaying partner by £252 in the tax year. Two conditions must be fulfilled:

- The spouse making the transfer has an income below the personal allowance, currently £12,570.

AND

- The person receiving the extra allowance pays basic rate tax but does not pay higher rate tax, which in 2022/23 begins at £50,270, except in Scotland where it begins at £46,631.

It is called marriage allowance. It applies to civil partners too, of course, but not to couples just living together in unofficial bliss.

If you get it this tax year 2022/23, you can also go back up to four years to 2018/19 and get the allowance for those years too. If so, you will get a cheque for £990, and £252 off your tax this year and in future years. If you claim successfully, the person transferring the tax allowance will have a tax code ending in N and the person receiving it will have a code ending in M.

Claiming should be simple – but it has been complicated by HMRC. Try first on the **gov.uk** website search 'marriage allowance'. But you will need a Government Gateway account. Alternatively, just call the helpline on 0300 200 3300. You will need your National Insurance number and that of your spouse and you will be asked some security questions. But it can be worthwhile as this email to me shows:

'My wife and I are indebted to you ... A couple of weeks ago, we followed your advice and contacted HMRC. Imagine our delight when yesterday a letter arrived with a cheque for £900!!!!!

And I believe my tax code will continue to be adjusted somewhat favourably in future years.

So, a huge thank you to you for making us aware of this opportunity, which has proved to be so beneficial to us!'

Mike and Christine, via email

MARRIED COUPLE'S ALLOWANCE

If one of you was born before 6 April 1935 – so you are around 88 or older – then you cannot claim marriage allowance. Instead, you can claim something much better – ta-da – the married couple's allowance. This can be worth up to £912.50 for the tax year and cannot be worth less than £353. Again, you can go back up to four tax years if you qualified in those years, more than quadrupling that amount in the year you claim. You do that by calling 0300 200 3300 with details of your marriage or civil partnership ceremony and the name and date of birth of your spouse. National Insurance numbers are always helpful but don't worry if they are not to hand.

Also, remember that whatever your age if you are blind then you get an extra £2600 allowance added to your personal allowance, cutting your tax by £520 this year, and probably a bit more in 2023/24.

POWER OF ATTORNEY

Before you die, you might lose your marbles. Who will deal with things if you do? By 'marbles' I mean what lawyers call 'mental capacity'. The ability to make decisions about your money and your medical treatment. For most of our life it is something we take for granted. But the longer we live, the more likely we are to lose that ability. About one in 14 over-65s have dementia and that rises to one in six of those over 80. So, although it is not as certain as death, there is a good chance it will affect us. Dementia, by the way, is the general term – Alzheimer's (named after Dr Alois Alzheimer who first identified it in 1906) is the most common cause of it but not the only one. It is also possible that we will have a stroke or an accident that causes brain damage.

That is why it is important to give someone we love and trust the power to make important life decisions for us while we still have the capacity to do so. To do that we make what is called a power of attorney. It is a big step. It can cause rifts in families. Denzil Lush, a former Senior Judge at the Court of Protection – which among other things picks up the pieces when a power of attorney goes wrong – wrote in a foreword to his 2017 book on powers of attorney that he would never sign one because of those risks. But don't let that put you off.

How to appoint them

The process is simple to describe. You sign a form saying that if you are unable to make decisions for yourself then one or more named people can act for you. You give the power – so you are called the 'donor' – they take it and are called the 'attorney'. The law is very strict about what they do – they must act only in your best interests. They cannot take or use your money or assets for themselves. Of course, if you live with them the line can be blurry. Are they allowed to use your money to build an extension for you to live in that boosts the value of their home? Yes. Are they allowed to take you on holiday with several family members using your money? Probably yes. Are they allowed to use your money to have a spa treatment and buy clothes, which, they say, will make them feel better and be a better carer? Certainly not. Can they use your money to go on holiday without you? No.

Financial instructions

Suppose you had a pension fund that you were drawing down at so much a year. The trustees of the fund need your instructions about investing that money and how much to take out for you each year. Once you lose mental capacity, you cannot give them instructions. That is where the person with the power of attorney steps in. And, again, every instruction they give must be in your best interests not theirs.

Your health

If they act in health matters that must also only be in your best interests. It helps them if you have indicated your wishes about medical treatment, such as operations, drugs and resuscitation – preferably in writing – to avoid arguments later. If they have the power, they can make those decisions for you if that decision is in your – not their – best interests.

Who do you choose?

It is vital to choose the right person or people to have this absolute power over your money and your health. Most of us have more than one relative or friend. But the number of people who have a power of attorney is normally limited to two or three – it can get unwieldy with more. What happens when the relatives without the power disagree with those who have it? Those disputes are decided by the Court of Protection, which can dismiss people as attorneys and take over the power to make decisions for the person lacking mental capacity.

Denzil Lush, as a former head judge at the Court, believes it does that well. But once the Court steps in, the charges can be high and the procedures slow. It also steps in if someone loses their mental capacity but has not made a power of attorney. In Scotland, that job is done by the Office of the Public Guardian and it is the Office of Care and Protection in Northern Ireland. They will appoint a person called a guardian (a controller in NI) to look after your affairs. It can even be the same relative you would have appointed as your attorney. Or it can be a professional, usually a lawyer, who does this job. They, of course, have to be paid.

In England and Wales, you can make a power of attorney yourself without paying anyone to do it for you. There are two powers, each covering different things:

- property and financial affairs
- health and welfare

You can make either or both.

You can do it all online or download the forms from **gov.uk** and fill them in yourself. If you are thinking of doing it, then it is a good idea to download the forms even if you get a solicitor to help. If you feel you need help, I would always recommend a solicitor. If they get it wrong you (or your heirs) can get redress. That is not true of other professionals who may do it for you. In Scotland and Northern Ireland, you should always use a solicitor.

The fee to register a Lasting Power of Attorney yourself is £82 per power – health and money – in England and Wales. In Scotland, it is £81 for both – called continuing and health. In Northern Ireland, it is £151 for an Enduring Power of Attorney. Fees can be reduced if your income is low and people on certain benefits are exempt. A solicitor may charge around £500 to do the job but prices vary widely.

And while you're at it, if you have not made a will yet go back to page 186 in Chapter 7 and see why it is a very good idea. You might even get a reduction from the lawyer if you do powers of attorney and a will at the same time.

Find out more at:

- **gov.uk** and search 'lasting power of attorney'
- **publicguardian-scotland.gov.uk** and search 'power of attorney'
- **nidirect.gov.uk** and search 'enduring power of attorney'

FUNERAL PLANS

I am not a fan of funeral plans. For more reasons than there is room for in this book. The idea of them is that you pay money now into a scheme, usually run by a funeral company, and when you die you are guaranteed a funeral for the price you have paid. In the past, the cost of funerals rose faster than inflation and they were sold as a good deal for your grieving relatives, who would have one less thing to worry about when you popped off.

But funeral plans were so risky and such bad value that two regulators stepped in. In September 2020, the Competition and Markets Authority made sure that prices were properly displayed, easy to find and explained clearly what was and was not covered in the plan. And the Financial Conduct Authority took over their regulation from the end of July 2022. As a result, many firms left the market and those that remain should be a lot better. But I still don't like or recommend them.

First, there is no need for one in most cases. If you will leave at least a few thousand pounds when you die, your heirs can pay the costs out of that. Your funeral is, by law, the first call on your estate. So, there is no need for you to set aside money specifically. And if you won't leave enough to pay for a funeral, then you should certainly not be putting aside money you can ill afford to pay for your death celebrations, which could be used to give you a better life while you have one.

Secondly, your funeral is not for you. It is for the living who grieve you. So, it is up to them what send-off you get and how much they spend on it. Of course, leave a note saying what you want (see 'letter of wishes' on page.190 in Chapter 7). But do not try to impose your wishes on others. You may well only pay for something far simpler than they would like, leaving them with the dilemma of what to do and what extra costs to incur. Or of course it may be the opposite. They may hate the horse-drawn glass carriage carrying a solid oak coffin led by a man waving a stick who doesn't speak. The funeral is for them. Let them decide. Or you could just leave your body to science and let your relatives arrange a memorial. One place that coordinates such gifts is the London Anatomy Office at kcl.ac.uk/research/london-anatomy-office.

DEBTS WHEN YOU DIE

Do debts die with you? The answer is simple: yes and no! All your assets are assembled by your executors and they also have to add up all your debts – or what are called lawful debts. That means debts that can be enforced. Ronnie from down the road may say what about that £20 I lent her last year but if there is no contract, then the debt should not be paid. The first call on the assets is your funeral expenses. After that, if the assets run out before the lawful debts are paid, then the remaining debts die with you. Relatives cannot be expected to pay them and should not do so. Look at it like this. You're born with nothing so if you die in debt, you're ahead in the game of life!

Joint debts

The one big exception is any joint debts – a mortgage with a partner or a joint loan. In that case, the survivor becomes liable for the whole debt – not half of it! The same is true if someone acted as a guarantor for a loan you had. If that debt cannot be paid out of the estate, then the person who acted as guarantor will be liable.

Credit cards are different. You cannot have a joint credit card. The account will be in one person's name even if there is another person who has a card on that account. That joint user is not liable for any debt left on the card. That is paid out of the estate, and only if there is enough to do so.

Joint bank accounts and jointly owned property, such as your home, pass immediately to your spouse or civil partner without formality through what is called 'survivorship'. Creditors find it very difficult to recover any debts from that money or property and any such claim should be resisted. Creditors can normally only recover debts from parts of the estate that were not jointly owned.

State pension on death

The same rules apply to pensions and benefits. When someone dies the death has to be reported within five days – eight in Scotland – by a relative or someone present at the death. There is a service called 'tell us once' that should ensure all government agencies are informed about the death. However, the Department for Work and Pensions is usually a bit slow in stopping a state pension. And it will try to recover any pension paid after the death. It has no right to this money and any letter asking for it should be ignored.

You may feel of course there is a moral obligation to pay it back. But beware. If you are the executor, your job is to pay lawful debts – not money to anyone who asks for it, whether that is £20 to Joe down the pub or £481 to the DWP. In 2020/21, it asked 195,700 people to repay money they did not owe and that year it recovered a total of £29 million, much of it from letters sent the previous year. I have been writing about this scandal for some years and am delighted that figure has almost halved from the £53 million recovered in 2017/18. The danger is that if you pay money out of the estate that is not legally recoverable, the heirs could make you pay that amount into the estate before it is divided up.

NOTE Solicitors often get this wrong and pay.

If the person who has died owned money to the DWP before their death, then it probably can recover that. But always challenge it and ask what powers it is using. More information on my blog (paullewismoney.blogspot.com) – search 'enforce demands'.

CARE HOME FEES

A great fear of people as they hit their seventies is that they will have to sell their home to pay for their care in old age. But most of us never go into a care home. There are only about 360,000 older people in long-term care or nursing homes out of 12 million people aged 66 or more. Most of us die at home or in hospital. The chances are at least two to one that you will never go into one.

And even if you do go into a care home, you won't have to sell your home to pay the fees. And, yes, I know the sister of Mrs Miggins who lives down the road did just that. But no-one ever actually has to do it. Some are misled into doing it. Some choose to do it. But no-one can be forced to do it.

Before I explain the rules, let us look at people who choose to do it.

You have a house worth, say, £250,000. When you go into care it will be empty (if it isn't because your partner or a relative over 60 lives there, then its value is ignored so you don't even need to think of selling it). If you sell it, you can use that £250,000 to buy the best care there is and live what time you have left (on average 2½ years) in the most comfort you can buy and you keep your pensions and other income to spend on who or what you want. Chances are you can claim extra income through attendance allowance (see page 253). However, if you do not sell it you are committed to letting the local council find a care home for you and taking all your income except £25.65 a week. I know which I would choose.

You do not have to sell your home if you don't want to, even if it is empty. You let the council find you a care home. You say you want a deferred payment agreement. The council says you cannot do that as you have more than £23,500 in the bank. So, you pay the fees until you have less and then you ask for a deferred payment agreement. You still give all your income towards the fees except £25.65 a week. You have to contribute a small amount from your savings, starting at £36 a week, then falling every few months. The rest of the bill clocks up, interest is charged and the debt is paid after your death by your heirs, probably from selling your home. I would still prefer selling it while I am alive and getting the best care I can afford.

Free care

The rules may change from October 2023 or the changes which would cost the government about £1 billion a year may be deferred. Before I explain those, you may not have to pay for your care at all. The NHS may pay in full. It works like this. When someone needs care, the local authority assesses them. If it decides residential or nursing home care is needed, then (outside Scotland) the individual should be considered for 'continuing healthcare' paid for by the NHS. That should always happen, especially if the person has gone straight from hospital into a nursing home. If their principal need is physical or mental health rather than personal care, then the NHS should continue to pay for it in full and without regard to their income or savings. Distinguishing between personal care and medical care is difficult. After all, if you are incontinent and you are not given the personal care that it requires, your condition would soon turn into a medical emergency. It is especially hard to say what is a medical need with a degenerative mental disease like Alzheimer's. But there comes a point where the need is mainly medical and at that stage the NHS should pay. In Scotland, it is called Hospital Based Complex Clinical Care and is very different.

If the council says you need a nursing home rather than a care home, and continuing healthcare has been refused, then you should ask if you are eligible for an NHS contribution of £187.60 a week towards that. Both things are decided by an NHS body called the Clinical Commissioning Group.

New rules possibly from October 2023

From October 2023 in England (Scotland, Wales and Northern Ireland are still considering their plans) the rules about paying for care may change.

The Johnson government promised that from October 2023 anyone going into care at that time will not be expected to pay more than £86,000 towards their care. That number came as one of those political bargains between Prime Minister Johnson, who wanted a lower figure, and Chancellor of the Exchequer Sunak, who wanted a higher one. That same Rishi

Sunak became Prime Minister towards the end of October 2022 so there may be changes in these plans. The idea is that once you have spent £86,000, the state will step in and pay the rest for as long as you need it. Sadly, it is not true. Most people will have to pay a lot more than that before the state steps in and will still have to carry on paying after it does:

- **The £86,000 cap is on the cost of care only.** The so-called hotel charges of bed and board in the home do not count towards it. Those have been fixed by the government at £200 a week in 2021, but by the time the changes come in it may well be around £220 a week or more. The cost of these hotel charges does not count towards the cap and even if the cap is reached, you will still have to pay them until you die.
- **The £86,000 cap is not on the actual cost of care you pay.** It is the cost of what the council would be willing to pay for the care you need. So, if your home says we are charging £800 a week for the care but the local authority says it would only be paying the home £550 a week for that, then only £550 counts towards the cap. So, out of your £1000 a week fee (£800 + £200 hotel fee) then only £550 a week would count towards the cap. So instead of reaching the cap after 86 weeks, it would take 156 weeks, longer than most people live once they have gone into a home.
- **There is another wrinkle in the sums.** Anything you use to pay for the fees that comes from a state benefit, such as income support, attendance allowance or pension credit, does not count towards the fees. So, if you have £100 of state benefits taken to pay for your fees that does not count towards the cap. Nor does anything paid by relatives or you in top-up fees – extra money to give you better conditions.

The overall effect is hard to calculate at this stage. But preliminary calculations indicate that it could take three or four years to reach the cap – longer than the average lifetime in a home of around 2½ years. By then the individual would have spent around double the £86,000 cap and would still be paying £20,000 to £30,000 a year after that.

The promise that once you have paid your care or nursing home £86,000, then the state would pay the rest is simply untrue. Absolutely.

One good thing about the plans is that in England you would be able to keep up to £100,000 of any savings you have. Once they are down to that level – it is currently £23,500 – the council should start to pay some of your care costs, and all of them when it falls to £20,000.

Protecting your home

Despite all this many people do want to 'protect' their home from the local authority means-test so they can leave it to their children. Some people think the way to do that is to give it to them and then carry on living there. This wheeze does not work any more than it does for inheritance tax. It is defeated by a rule called 'deliberate deprivation of assets'. If you take any steps to get rid of something you own and at least part of your motivation is to increase your entitlement to help from public funds, then the asset can still be counted as yours. In other words, even if your home is owned by your children, the local council could count it as if it was yours and refuse to pay your care home fees.

However, if you are a couple there are two ways to own a home together. The first is called 'joint tenancy', which despite its name is about how you own your own home. With joint tenancy, you each own all of it. When one of the couple dies, the home simply passes to the survivor.

The other way of owning a home is as 'tenants in common'. If you do that, then you each own half the property – or it can be a different share if you want but let's stick with half. When one dies, the other can leave their half to someone else, say your children. This avoids the 'deliberate deprivation' rule. If the surviving partner needs to go into a care home, the local council has a problem. What is the correct value of half a house when someone else has the right to live there? Probably zero. But there is a downside. The other half is owned by our children. Any one of them, as part owner, could force a sale of the home. And although I am sure you trust your children and they love you very much, the decision might be taken from their hands. If one of them divorces, then their share of your home will be in the settlement and a sale could be forced by the court. The same is true if one of them goes bankrupt. So, the surviving parent would have no real security and the chances are would never go into a care home anyway.

DO NOT TOUCH – Hiding schemes

As I said, the great majority of us do not go into a care home. And if we do and our home is empty, we do not have to sell it to pay for care while we are alive. But people are afraid of care home costs and especially afraid of 'losing' their home to pay them. Some firms take advantage of those fears and desires by selling schemes to people to protect the value of their home from the care home means-test. They make exaggerated claims about the risk of losing your home and the number of people affected. The schemes are usually sold at meetings in hotels or other venues to crowds of anxious people in their sixties and seventies. The schemes are supposed to work by putting your home into a trust, which is a legal device so the property is actually owned not by you but by the trust. The theory is that as you no longer own the property it will escape being counted as your asset when the means-test is applied. They will charge you thousands of pounds.

Of course, it does not work. The 'deliberate deprivation of assets' rule can be used by the local authority to ignore the fact that the home is in trust. So even if your home was owned by a trust, the local council could count it as if it was yours and refuse to pay your care home fees.

Buying a scheme of this sort is money down the drain – or rather commission into the pocket of the person who sold it to you. The firms selling these schemes are unregulated and there is nowhere to go to with a complaint.

Even worse when you do die – in or out of a care home – your heirs may have to pay extra fees to take your home out of the trust before it can form part of your estate.

Sue emailed Money Box *about her father-in-law who had died aged 92 and never gone into a care home.*

'We found a Home Protection Trust, *which he had paid £2000 to set up to avoid paying for care needs. Our problem is that if we want to sell the house we need a deed of appointment, which will cost £750+vat. He was 88 years old when this was set up. I feel older people are easy prey for people who make easy money from these people who are trying to protect their savings.'*

Sue, via email

Remember:

- Don't be afraid of care costs.
- If your spouse or an elderly relative lives in your house, it won't be counted.
- If your home is empty, ask for a deferred payment agreement.
- If you have a valuable home, why not sell it and buy yourself the best care you can get?
- Never try to avoid care home costs.

CHAPTER 10

TO INFINITY AND BEYOND

NO REGRETS

GO BACK IN TIME!

OK, OK. You've made it. The music of life is over – and incidentally you know that music you picked for the funeral? They didn't play it. Some thought it too glum. But your niece – John's girl – said it was too cheerful and it would trigger her. So, it was just a few hymns (I know you hate hymns, so did they) and then the sound of weeping. And, look, I don't want to be mean but some of that weeping was not because they miss you (though they do. Of course. Honestly. Especially your humour/kindness/sense of fun – delete as applicable). But they are really weeping because ...

YOU DIDN'T MAKE A WILL!

Look. We did wills in Chapter 7. Did you bother? No. What? You didn't think you would ever die? Or not just yet anyway. That is the thing about the Grim Reaper. His scythe is silent. If you do not make a will, the worst-case scenario is that the Prince of Wales gets everything. Honestly. He can. And OK it does depend which bit of the UK you live in – it might be the Duke of Lancaster aka the Monarch. And of course, they may not need or even want it but that is how it works in a monarchy.

Thanks to more sensible and recent laws, it usually goes to your nearest and dearest and that is OK and you may think fine, why bother? But if most of your close relatives have already died it is conceivable that the whole lot will go to your nephew's second wife's stepson, who you met once and you wouldn't even want to give him a cold chip that you couldn't eat yourself.

YOU ASKED THE BANK TO DO THE PROBATE!

Do you think they've got your money to burn! I warned about this in Chapter 7 too (see page 189). Pick a relative who is sensible. Almost anyone can do it. Honest.

YOU HAVEN'T LEFT YOUR PASSWORDS!

Yes. Yes. You should not make passwords that anyone can guess. 123456 is not a good idea. And even ones you think those intimate with you would guess, they probably wouldn't. And no, you should not make passwords so complicated that you can't remember them. And I know you are told never to write them down. But I am going to tell you now – you should have written them down! At least the one to unlock your computer. Because without that, they cannot even find your …

DYING TIDILY LETTER

What? You didn't write a dying tidily letter? How are they supposed to know what to do with your collection of Jimmy Choos? Or those rare old potato peelers – some dating back to the 1840s – that you inherited from your dad and always claimed would pay for your funeral? You said you knew someone who would buy them! Who???

Here is a picture of a wormhole.

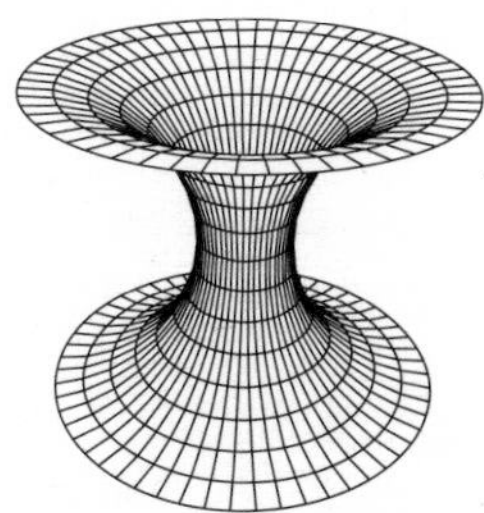

Crawl back through it now and make a will, write a letter of wishes and that dying tidily letter before you get to Chapter 10.

And coming back to passwords – wormholes allow you to land anywhere – security experts say that writing one down in ink on a piece of paper and then hiding it is actually both safe and secure. You can't hack a piece of paper. Then those who come after you can unlock the riches of your hard drive. Including that dying tidily letter you are just about to go and write now you have finished this book.

I would say 'take care', but I hope you have done that already.

GLOSSARY

Brief definitions of some common financial terms

Actuary – a mathematician who works out the likelihood of future events and what they will cost.

Additional rate tax – the top rate of income tax of 45% on income over £150,000. In Scotland it is 46%.

Alternative dispute resolution (ADR) services – an ombudsman service where customers can take disputes with firms to get them sorted. Some are better than others.

Annuity – you give an insurance company a lump sum and it gives you an income for life in exchange.

Attendance allowance – a weekly benefit for people aged 66 or more, who need help from someone else with their daily lives.

Auto-enrolment – a pension scheme set up by an employer, which almost all employees automatically pay into unless they opt out.

Basic rate tax – the rate of income tax charged on income over your personal allowance. Currently it is 20%. Plans announced in September 2022 to cut it to 19% were abandoned indefinitely in October. In Scotland a lower starter rate applies on a narrow band of income.

Best Start food payments – paid in Scotland in addition to a Best Start grant to help with healthy food in pregnancy and until the child is three.

Best Start grants – paid in Scotland to a mother if she gets certain means-tested benefits when she is pregnant and then when the child is at school.

Budget – statement by the Chancellor of the Exchequer that sets out their plans for tax in future years. Usually happens once a year, sometimes more often.

Budgeting – managing your income and expenditure so you know what you can afford to spend and how your money will last.

Capital gains tax – a tax on the rise in the value of something you own, usually charged when you sell it or give it away.

Carer's allowance – a weekly payment to someone who cares for a person who gets certain disability benefits.

Chancellor, Chancellor of the Exchequer – the government minister in charge of fixing tax and the economy. Some tax powers are devolved to ministers in Scotland and Wales.

Chargeback – if you buy something on a debit card and it goes wrong you should be able to get your money back from your bank. Less certain and more complicated than Section 75 protection.

Child tax credit – a means-tested benefit for people in work who have children. Being replaced by universal credit.

Child trust funds – a government-funded scheme for every child born from 1 September 2002 to 2 January 2011. They can take the money out when they reach 18.

Civil partnership – a legal arrangement like marriage but with a different name and all the same advantages and disadvantages.

Commission – money paid to a salesperson or adviser for selling a product, usually a percentage of the purchase price. Banned for sales of investments and pensions but still found on sales of insurance and mortgages.

Common-law wife or husband – popular phrase for two people who live together as a couple but are not married or civil partners. They generally have almost no legal rights over each other's money or property. The rules are slightly different in Scotland.

Consumer Prices Index (CPI) – the official estimate of the rate at which prices are rising.

Continuous payment authority – permission for a business to take regular payments from a credit or debit card. Often taken out without realising it. Can be cancelled at your bank.

Credit card – a card to buy things with but every penny is borrowed. Interest is charged and a monthly payment is required.

Credit score – a number that is supposed to show lenders how good a risk you are. If you miss payments on loans your credit score will get worse.

Current account – an account with a bank to receive and manage your money. Only use a regulated bank for this job.

Debit card – a card that is used to spend money from your current account.

Deferred payment agreement – an arrangement with the local council so people in care homes can have their fees paid from their estate after they die.

Defined benefit (DB) pension – pays a proportion of your pay for every year you have paid in. Also called a final salary or career average pension.

Defined contribution (DC) pension – a pension scheme that saves your contributions and those of your employer in your own pot. When you retire you can take it out or use it to provide an income.

Deliberate deprivation of assets – giving up an asset, such as a house, a valuable item or money, to make yourself eligible to help from the state. A bad idea as it doesn't work.

Direct debit – an agreement with a firm to take money out of your current account as and when it chooses.

Direct Debit Guarantee – if money is wrongly taken by a direct debit your bank must reimburse you swiftly.

Drawdown – an arrangement to take money, usually regular amounts, from a pension pot. Also used for money taken out in lumpsums from an Equity release plan.

Equity release – a product that allows older people to take a cash sum from the value of their home, which is not repaid until they die.

ESG (Environmental, Social, Governance) – a fashionable term for investments in firms that do good rather than harm. Often misused.

Estate – a posh word for everything you leave when you die – however much or little it is!

Ethical investing – an investment that only buys shares in firms that are ethical – you can decide what that means to you.

Executor – the person you choose to ensure your property and money is sorted out after you die as stated in your will.

Final salary pension – a type of defined benefit pension that pays you a fraction of the pay you earned in the year before you retired.

Financial Conduct Authority (FCA) – the official body that regulates banks and most financial firms that deal in investments, pensions, mortgages, loans, savings and other financial products.

Financial Ombudsman Service – the official body that deals with complaints by customers about regulated financial firms. Can award compensation.

Financial Services Compensation Scheme (FSCS) – the official body that pays compensation due to customers of firms that have gone out of business.

FTSE – an abbreviation for several indexes that track the value of shares in public companies on the London Stock Exchange.

Gift Aid – a way to make a donation to a charity that boosts the value of it by 25% if the donor pays income tax.

Gift with reservation of benefit (GROB) – a gift to someone where the donor still keeps the benefit of it – like giving away your house but still living in it. Not a good idea.

Government Gateway account – the way to access most government services, such as tax and childcare.

Guarantor – a person who agrees to pay a debt or payments on a loan for someone else if they don't do it. This should be avoided.

Healthy Start card – given by the NHS to pregnant women and mothers with a child aged under 4 who are on universal credit or other means-tested benefits and on low incomes to help them buy healthy food and vitamins.

His Majesty's Revenue & Customs (HMRC) – also called the taxman (though many are women) or the Revenue. The department that collects all national taxes, including income tax and VAT.

High income child benefit charge – a tax on child benefit where one partner has an income over £50,000 a year. Can wipe out the child benefit.

Higher rate tax – a tax of 40p in the pound on income above a certain amount. In Scotland it is 41p and it begins at a lower amount.

Housing benefit – money from the local council to pay some of your rent if your income is low. In Northern Ireland it can also pay some of your rates.

Income support – an old means-tested benefit, which is being replaced by universal credit.

Income-based jobseeker's allowance – a means-tested benefit for people looking for work. It is being replaced by universal credit.

Income-related employment and support allowance – a means-tested benefit for people who can't work due to ill health or disability. This is largely being replaced by universal credit.

Independent financial adviser (IFA) – a qualified and regulated financial adviser who is independent of any products or firms and will find you the best from the whole market. The only sort of adviser to use.

Index-linked pension – a company or private pension that rises with inflation, though that rise is often limited if inflation is high.

Inflation – the general rise in prices over a year published by the Office for National Statistics. The Consumer Prices Index (CPI) is the usual way it is measured.

Inheritance tax – a tax on the value of money and property someone leaves when they die.

Interest – a charge on a loan paid as a percentage of the amount borrowed. Also paid on savings as a percentage of the amount saved.

Intestacy – dying without leaving a will. Not a good idea as your property and money are divided up according to strict legal rules and may not go where you want them to go.

ISA – Individual Savings Account, where the interest and growth of the money is free of tax.

JISA – an ISA (see above) for a child, hence Junior ISA.

Letter of wishes – a letter written to accompany a will expressing the wishes of the deceased. It has no legal force.

Marriage allowance – a tax allowance for a married person (or civil partner) whose spouse has too low an income to pay tax on it.

Married couple's allowance – a tax allowance for a married person (or civil partner) where at least one spouse was born before 6 April 1935. Worth more than marriage allowance and paid instead of it.

Maternity allowance – a weekly payment to women who take time off working because they are pregnant or have a new baby but do not get maternity pay from an employer.

Means-tested benefits – weekly or monthly money from the state that is related to your income and savings.

Minimum wage – the minimum rate per hour an employer must pay. Varies by age and changes every April.

National Insurance – a tax on earnings that also gives entitlement to the state pension and some benefits.

National Living Wage – the name for the minimum wage paid to people aged 23 or more.

National Savings & Investments (NS&I) – government savings institution where your money generally earns poor interest but is 100% safe.

New-style employment and support allowance – if you are unable to work due to ill health or disability you can claim this benefit based on your National Insurance contributions. Normally lasts for twelve months but can be longer. Not means-tested.

New-style jobseeker's allowance – if you are out of work but actively seeking a job you can claim this benefit for six months based on your National Insurance contributions. Not means-tested.

NFTs or non-fungible tokens (NFTs) – things that don't exist but have an electronic record to say they do and are sold to you for real money that does exist.

Ombudsman – a person or office that takes complaints from customers and can order redress or compensation.

Overdraft/overdrawn – a negative bank balance. If you have £60 in your current account and you take out £100 from a cash machine, you are £40 overdrawn. Interest will be charged.

Pay As You Earn (PAYE) – the method used by HMRC to collect income tax and National Insurance contributions from people in work.

Pension credit – a means-tested benefit for people aged 66 or more to top up their income. Couples must both be 66 or more.

Power of attorney – permission for someone else to run your financial or health affairs when you can no longer do so.

Premium bonds – a savings product from NS&I. Your capital is safe but the interest is put into a prize pool and paid out each month as £25 or higher prizes to randomly chosen bonds.

Prenup or pre-nuptial agreement – made before a marriage or civil partnership to protect money or assets owned by one partner by limiting the other's rights if the marriage or civil partnership ends.

Pre-paid card – a plastic card used to spend money that is pre-loaded onto the card. Can be expensive.

Probate – the formal approval of the distribution of a deceased person's money and property.

Register office – the office where births, marriages or civil partnerships, and deaths are registered. Often wrongly called a 'registry office'.

Registrar – a person in the register office who is authorised to marry people and fill in birth, marriage, civil partnership and death certificates.

Retail Prices Index (RPI) – an older way of measuring inflation, which always shows a higher rate of price rises than the Consumer Prices Index.

Section 75 protection – if you pay by credit card for something costing over £100 you get extra protection if it goes wrong or is a fraud.

Self-employed – someone who works for themselves not for an employer.

Self-Invested Personal Pension (SIPP) – a pension pot you save money into and make your own decision about how it is invested.

Shared parental leave (SPL) – mothers and fathers and same-sex couples can now share the rights to time off for a new child.

Sharia financial products – loans, investments or savings that conform to the standards of Islam. No interest can be involved and some unethical products are excluded from investments.

Standing order – an instruction to your bank to pay someone or a firm a regular fixed amount.

Statutory maternity pay – the amount an employer has to pay to a new mother and for a few weeks before the birth.

Statutory paid paternity leave – a father can now have some time off with limited pay for a new child.

Statutory shared parental pay – mothers and fathers and same-sex couples can share some of the pay received by a new parent.

Statutory sick pay (SSP) – a payment from an employer to someone who is off sick.

Stock market or stock exchange – the place where shares in companies are bought and sold.

Sure Start maternity grant – a payment for a first child to a parent who gets a means-tested benefit.

Tax allowance – an amount of money on which tax – usually income tax – is not paid.

Tax avoidance schemes – any scheme that tries to reduce tax due by bending the rules. Can end up very expensive.

Tax code – digits and letters that tell an employer how much tax to deduct under PAYE.

The Treasury – the government department that deals with financial matters.

Trading Standards – has offices throughout England, Scotland and Wales that enforce the law about how things are sold.

Triple lock – a promise made by politicians to increase the main part of the state pension each year by earnings, prices or 2.5%, whichever is biggest. Sometimes broken and may not last much longer.

Trust – a legal arrangement for someone else to manage your assets, often used to reduce tax – or try to – or protect assets for someone who cannot do that themselves.

Will – the legal document that sets out what will happen to your money and property when you die. There are strict rules about how a will is written and signed. The rules are different in Scotland.

Working tax credit – a means-tested benefit for people in work. Being replaced by universal credit.

WEBSITES AND RESOURCES

Chapter 1: Birth and before

Turn2us: **turn2us.org.uk**

Working Families: **workingfamilies.org.uk**

United Kingdom Government website: **gov.uk**

Scottish Government website: **mygov.scot**

Northern Ireland Government website: **nidirect.gov.uk**

Welsh Government website: **gov.wales**

Healthy Start card: **healthystart.nhs.uk**

Child benefit calculator: **gov.uk/child-benefit-tax-calculator**

Benefits calculator: **entitledto.co.uk**

Chapter 2: Childhood 1–11

United Kingdom Government childcare website: **childcarechoices.gov.uk**

Childcare calculator: **gov.uk/childcare-calculator**

Universal credits calculator: **benefits-calculator.turn2us.org.uk**

Wales Government childcare website: **childcareinformation.wales**

Northern Ireland Government childcare website: **www.nidirect.gov.uk/information-and-services/parenting-and-childcare/childcare**

United Kingdom Government childcare calculator: **gov.uk/childcare-calculator**

United Kingdom Government website: **gov.uk**

Kinship Carers: **kinship.org.uk**

Chapter 3: Teens 12–18

National insurance number: His Majesty's Revenue & Customs (HMRC) on 0300 200 3500

ACAS: **acas.org.uk/advice** or 0300 123 1100

Child Trust Fund finder: **findctf.sharefound.org**

Chartered Institute of Personnel and Development: **cipd.co.uk**

Social media

Financial Conduct Authority: **fca.org.uk**

Chapter 4: Starting out 18–23

How to Complain Helen Dewdney (The Complaining Cow, 2019)

Money Savings Expert mis-selling of packaged bank accounts: **moneysavingexpert.com/reclaim/reclaim-packaged-bank-accounts**

Paul Lewis blog: **paullewismoney.blogspot.com**

United Kingdom Government website: **gov.uk**

Love and money

Surviving Economic Abuse: **survivingeconomicabuse.org**

Chapter 5: The working world 23–41

Money Helper: **moneyhelper.org.uk/en/money-troubles/way-forward/bill-prioritiser**

National Debtline: **nationaldebtline.org**

StepChange Debt Charity: **stepchange.org**

GamCare: **gamcare.org.uk**

Gamblers Anonymous: **gamblersanonymous.org.uk**

Citizens Advice: **citizensadvice.org.uk**

Paul Lewis blog: **paullewismoney.blogspot.com**

Benefits calculator: **entitledto.co.uk**

Fraud klaxon

The Contingent Reimbursement Model (CRM) Code: **lendingstandardsboard.org.uk/crm-code**

Financial Conduct Authority: **fca.org.uk**

Chapter 6: Spending 23–41

Leasehold Advisory Service's (LAS): **lease-advice.org**

L&C Mortgages: **landc.co.uk**

Water meter calculator: **ccwater.org.uk/watermetercalculator**

Which?: **which.co.uk**

UK International Consumer Centre: **ukecc.net**

How to complain

The Financial Ombudsman Service: **financial-ombudsman.org.uk**

Financial Services Compensation Scheme: **fscs.org.uk**

Ombudsmen covering telecoms and energy providers: **ombudsman-services.org**

Ombudsmen covering retail: **retailadr.org.uk**

Civil Aviation Authority: **caa.co.uk**

England and Wales small claims: **moneyclaim.gov.uk**

Scotland small claims: **scotscourts.gov.uk**

Northern Ireland small claims: **justice-ni.gov.uk**

CEO emails and phone numbers: **ceoemail.com**

United Kingdom Government website: **gov.uk**

How to Complain Helen Dewdney (The Complaining Cow, 2019)

Chapter 7: Getting sensible 41–60

Savings Champion: **savingschampion.co.uk**

Investing

Ian Cowie's 'Personal Account' in the Business and Money section of *The Sunday Times*

EIRIS: **eirisfoundation.org**

MoneyHelper: **moneyhelper.org.uk**

Pensions Advisory Service on 0300 123 1047

Pension Wise on 0300 330 1001

AdviserBook: **adviserbook.co.uk**

Unbiased: **unbiased.co.uk**

VouchedFor: **vouchedfor.co.uk**

Chapter 8: Preparing to wind down 55–70

United Kingdom Government website: **gov.uk**

HMRC's Taxes Helpline on 0300 200 3300

Pension Wise on 0800 138 3944

Pensions Advisory Service on 0800 011 3797

Life expectancy calculator: **ONS.gov.uk** search 'life expectancy calculator'

Paul Lewis blog: **paullewismoney.blogspot.com**

MoneyHelper: **comparison.moneyhelper.org.uk/en/guaranteed-income-for-life/quotes**

Chapter 9: Wound down 70–99

Benefits calculator: **entitledto.co.uk**

Pensions credit claim line: 0800 99 1234

Attendance allowance help: **independentage.org** or call 0330 021 2503

Attendance allowance help: **gov.uk** or call 0800 731 0122; in Northern Ireland 0800 587 0912

Marriage allowance help: **gov.uk** or call 0300 200 3300

Married couple's allowance help: call HMRC on 0300 200 3300

England and Wales power of attorney help: **gov.uk**

Scotland power of attorney help: **publicguardian-scotland.gov.uk**

Northern Ireland power of attorney help: **nidirect.gov.uk**

London Anatomy Office: **kcl.ac.uk/research/london-anatomy-office**

Paul Lewis blog: **paullewismoney.blogspot.com**

ACKNOWLEDGEMENTS

Don't worry – I'll keep it short and reading this page is not essential.

Over the years dozens and dozens of *Money Box* researchers, producers, editors and others have worked very hard to keep me sounding knowledgeable and intelligent. I thank them all and won't pick out any individual, except one. Alex Lewis (no relation) was series producer for some years before the programme moved to Salford. I mention her because it was she who came up with the structure for this book as a life journey. The moment she said it the people in the meeting all looked at each other and said that's brilliant. Which it was. I ran with it, and you can see the result here. Thank you, Alex.

Throughout my long career as a financial journalist I have come across the very worst and the very best in the financial industry – and of course, the vast majority who are in between. I am grateful to them all because every one of them has taught me a lot. The good ones know who they are. Thanks especially to them.

At Penguin Random House my editor Nell Warner had been wonderfully encouraging and positive even in the dark times and always full of calm, clear and helpful advice. Editor Shammah Banerjee made great improvements and peppered her changes with lovely comments such as 'I really LIKE this turn of phrase!' Kay Halsey has been what she has to be – pernickety – which I love and Karen Farrington was always helpful in the early stages. Thanks to them all.

Of course, any egregious solecisms, errors, missteps, transgressions, misapprehensions, misjudgements or plain rubbish are all, as they say, my bad.

Finally, my wonderful wife Emma Lynch. She told me which jokes to leave out and occasionally I followed her advice. As you will see, she is always right.

Paul Lewis

October 2022